THE FIRE STILL BURNS

THE FIRE
STILL
BURNS

REFLECTIONS
ON THE THEOLOGY AND PRACTICE OF THE
MINISTRY OF THE WORD AND SACRAMENTS
IN THE UNITED REFORMED CHURCH

STUART P. SCOTT

Matador
Unit E2 Airfield Business Park,
Harrison Road, Market Harborough,
Leicestershire. LE16 7UL
Tel: 0116 279 2299
Email: books@troubador.co.uk
Web: www.troubador.co.uk/matador
Twitter: @matadorbooks

ISBN 978 180313 248 8

British Library Cataloguing in Publication Data.
A catalogue record for this book is available from the British Library.

Printed and bound in the UK by TJ Books LTD, Padstow, Cornwall
Typeset in 11pt Minion Pro by Troubador Publishing Ltd, Leicester, UK

Matador is an imprint of Troubador Publishing Ltd

Dedicated to

- those through whom my call to the Ministry of the Word and Sacraments in the United Reformed Church was discerned: Bexley Congregational (to 1972) and then United Reformed Church, where the journey of faith began; the South Aston Church Centre, where I spent the year (1982–83) that changed my life, and the SAND volunteers; the Queens College, Birmingham, now the Queens Foundation for Ecumenical Theological Education, where I was trained for this Ministry (1983–86); and in particular memory and with gratitude for the friendship, support and encouragement of Hugh Kember, Peter Loveitt and Lesslie Newbigin
- local churches I have had the privilege of serving in Coventry (1986–91), Birmingham (1991–2000) and the Black Country (2001–16)
- colleagues in the Ministry of the Word and Sacraments I have served alongside, responding to God's call and offering ourselves in the service of Christ through the Church as the sign, instrument and foretaste of the kingdom of God
- all preparing and equipping those exploring and

developing a vocation as Ministers of the Word and Sacraments: colleagues in training and development roles, denominationally and ecumenically, and the staff and governors of the Resource Centres for Learning of the United Reformed Church in Cambridge, Manchester and Scotland

- Rebecca M, for the gift of friendship and hospitality since 1975
- Jan, and Rebecca and Jonathan and their partners and families, my companions in life, love and learning
- and to Mum and Dad: for your example in Christian lifelong learning and service and your constant love, encouragement and support

See, I am making all things new (Revelation 21:5, *NRSV*)

CONTENTS

ACKNOWLEDGEMENTS

I enjoyed the opportunity to spend the Michaelmas term 2019 on sabbatical leave in Westminster College, Cambridge, funded and supported by the Cheshunt Foundation, with additional support from the United Reformed Church and the Coward Trust. I offer my thanks to them all for this gift of time, and particularly to Sam White, then the Director of the Cheshunt Foundation. I thank also all students and staff at Westminster College for their hospitality and welcome, during that term and on numerous occasions before and since.

The first five reflections are the fruit of reading, conversations and reflection in that term and were written during the sabbatical leave and edited in early 2020. In March 2020 the United Kingdom went into lockdown as a result of the Covid-19 pandemic and the reflection on Ministry in the pandemic was written between May and December 2020, with further editing and the reflection "On Endings" added in 2021 and then final changes in 2022. I thank Robert Pope, Director of Studies in Church History and Doctrine at

Westminster College, for generously giving his time and his advice and guidance in the editing process.

Finally I thank all who shared their wisdom, insights, experience and stories during this journey of exploration and reflection, while acknowledging my final responsibility for the views and opinions expressed, conclusions drawn and any errors and omissions.

ONE

INTRODUCTION

"Take this moment, sign and space;
take my friends around;
here among us make the place
where Your love is found.

Take the time to call my name,
take the time to mend
who I am and what I've been,
all I've failed to tend.

Take the tiredness of my days,
take my past regret,
letting Your forgiveness touch
all I can't forget.

Take the little child in me,
scared of growing old;

help him/her here to find his/her worth
made in Christ's own mould.

Take my talents, take my skills,
take what's yet to be;
let my life be Yours, and yet,
let it still be me."[1]

I have no recollection of when these simple and yet powerful
words first came to my attention. They are copyrighted 1989,
three years after my ordination to Ministry of the Word and
Sacraments in the United Reformed Church. Looking back
over more than thirty years, with retirement on the horizon,
they reflect my journey of learning and discipleship, the
Ministry I have sought to offer, and offer still.

I have recently discovered the writing of poet and
Anglican priest Malcolm Guite, who has written several
books of poetry and others on Christian faith and theology.
He comments on how we discover God's blessing and
healing as prayer takes us deeper into ourselves, and into
our stories. Guite writes, *When we begin to pray, we have to
start where we are, usually just on the surface of our lives; but
there is always so much else going on. We all have a familiar
outer layer to our lives but are there not also, deeper in our
psyche, the burrows and dens where the shyer and more furtive
elements of our inner life are rooted and nestling? Might these
half-acknowledged parts of ourselves also be brought to God*

1   From the song 'Take This Moment'. Words by John L. Bell & Graham
    Maule. Copyright © 1989, 2000 WGRG, c/o Iona Community,
    Glasgow, Scotland. Reproduced by permission. www.wildgoose.scot

for blessing, noticed a little and offered to him? Do we have longer and deeper memories, perhaps going right back into our family histories, which have, as it were, shaped the landscape of who we are? Perhaps prayer might be a way to bring them for blessing and healing to God, for whom all times are present, in whom is the fulness of time.[2]

These reflections bring some of my own story to God for blessing and healing. They have been edited, developed and then extended to include reflection on Ministry through the Covid-19 pandemic and are offered to the wider Church to bring blessing as we journey in times of challenge and opportunity through and out of the pandemic and explore where God is calling us now.

This is not academic writing[3] although footnotes, references and a bibliography are included. I write from personal perspective to process recent experience and to reflect on the longer term and seek to draw from that experience for the wider Church. Each of the reflections stands alone but shares a common concern for the future of the United Reformed Church and the renewal of its local churches, focusing on the shape of Ministry that serves those churches. They also progress, from the past to the future.

The first reflection highlights issues and experience in a long Ministry at St John's United Reformed Church in Stourbridge. I was Minister there for fifteen years, from September 2001 to October 2016. I also give close

---

2 Guite, M. 2014 p.60.

3 I carry some scars of experience in that area – and refer to an unpublished associated thesis in due course.

attention to the closure of the church at New Year 2017. In the second reflection I offer thoughts on the theology and practice of Ministry of the Word and Sacraments. In the third I consider reports and resolutions related to ordained Ministry presented to the General Assembly of the United Reformed Church since 1982. I offer reflection on some numbers and some informal conversations around the theology and practice of ordained Ministry in the fourth reflection before reflecting in the fifth on the development of "pioneer ministry", mainly in the context of the United Reformed Church but with some reference to ecumenical partnership. I then present some preliminary conclusions, before the sixth reflection, on Ministry in the United Reformed Church in the coronavirus pandemic. The closure of the United Church, Halesowen in October 2021, against the background of the continuing pandemic, prompted the additional reflection "On endings" which I have inserted before final conclusions.

For much of the writing the working title was *Running Out of Years*. These words originated in an apparently off-hand comment the Director of the Black Country Radio made to me, when they were about to leave the St John's Stourbridge Church building for a purpose-built studio. His words were "We ran out years". They express a sense of frustration and lost opportunity, arising from the delays and resistance to proposals to adapt the building, and the church's apparent inability to make decisions. The closure of the radio studio was, it could be argued, significant for the life of the church, as a few months after the Radio Group left St John's in 2016 the church made its decision to close. Here, however, the words were intended to convey realism rather than pessimism. I hold in mind the apostle Paul's words in 2 Corinthians 4, the *treasure in clay jars* (2 Corinthians 4:7–9, *NRSV*), and *So we do not lose heart. Even though our outer nature is wasting away, our inner nature is being renewed day by day* (2 Corinthians 4:16, *NRSV*), and also the motto "*Nec tamen consumebatur*", found in many Presbyterian churches around the world. This motto is seen throughout Westminster College, in the old in nineteenth-century masonry and stained glass, and in the new in twenty-first-century artwork.

"*Nec tamen consumebatur*" is the Latin translation for Moses' experience recorded in Exodus 3:1–12. In the wilderness Moses is confronted by the burning bush: *the angel of the Lord appeared to him in a flame of fire out of a bush; he looked, and the bush was blazing, yet it was not consumed* (Exodus 3:2, *NRSV*). Neil Thorogood, former Principal at Westminster College, Cambridge, entitles his work containing these words, which is on display in the Cheshunt Room in the College, *Westminster DNA*. The title for the work is careful and deliberate.

A Google search gives these and similar answers to the questions "What is DNA?" and "What does DNA do?":

"Why is DNA so important? Put simply, DNA contains the instructions necessary for life."

"The code within our DNA provides directions on how to make proteins that are vital for our growth, development, and overall health."

"DNA stands for deoxyribonucleic acid. It's made up of units of biological building blocks called nucleotides."

"DNA is a vitally important molecule for not only humans, but for most other organisms as well. DNA contains our hereditary material and our genes – it's what makes us unique."[4]

"Virtually every cell in your body contains DNA or the genetic code that makes you *you*. DNA carries the instructions for the development, growth, reproduction, and functioning of all life."

"In short, DNA is a long molecule that contains each person's unique genetic code. It holds the instructions for building the proteins that are essential for our bodies to function."[5]

"The DNA code contains instructions needed to make the proteins and molecules essential for our growth, development and health."[6]

Thorogood himself says "Westminster College, Cambridge, has been my place of work and a huge part of my life since 2005. It is a glorious Victorian and art deco masterpiece that sits at the end of one of Cambridge's great vistas, rising out of the trees. The building is a host of reds and browns with all of its brickwork and wood. There's a little bit of gold for the emblem of the burning bush that stopped Moses in the wilderness which adorns our gates. And I've included the scrambled letters of our college motto: *Nec Tamen*

---

4   https://www.healthline.com/health/what-is-dna#what-is-dna [accessed 7th January 2022].

5   https://www.medicalnewstoday.com/articles/319818 [accessed 7th January 2022].

6   https://www.yourgenome.org/facts/what-does-dna-do [accessed 7th January 2022].

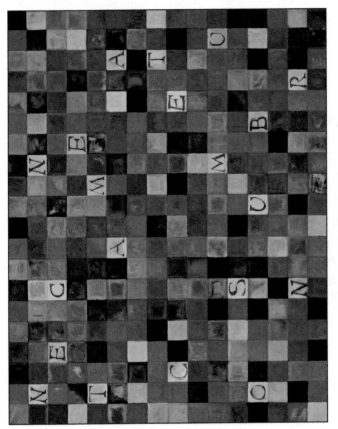

Westminster DNA Neil Thorogood
©Neil Thorogood (reproduced with permission of the artist)

Consumebatur – 'and it was not consumed'. God's fire of faith and holiness still burns bright and glorious, and will never be extinguished. But I've jumbled the letters, because this is a place where folk learn about theology and ministry and there's plenty to untangle!"[7]

In the course of time, and in the light of the planning for the celebrations of the fiftieth birthday of the United Reformed Church in 2022, I changed the title of this publication to the more positive "*The Fire Still Burns*", but I will suggest in these reflections that neither deployment of current Ministry, nor a new shape of Ministry, will result necessarily in the renewal of local churches and the United Reformed Church in particular. Time and again it will be said that in the life of the Church there are no quick fixes, no simple solutions. It is however the case that, if you keep on doing the same thing, you are likely to get the same result. There are strong arguments for experiment and change. The continual challenge to the Church, in this as in every age, is to discern the leading of the Holy Spirit and to respond in using the gifts with which the Spirit equips and empowers the Church. The renewal of the Church is always the action of the Holy Spirit. It is the Church's task to listen to what God is saying, and to respond to God's call in faith and obedience. There may be no "solutions" as such, and I certainly would not presume, on the basis of a few months' reflection, to offer a path to renewal for the denomination I serve. I will

---

7 https://www.neilthorogood.com/photo_9856828.html [accessed 26th November 2021]. I spent a term studying Hebrew for three hours a week in the Cheshunt Room at the college and only succeeded in deciphering the text in my final week!

however suggest these areas for urgent attention and action at such a time as this: leadership as it is exercised in the United Reformed Church, relationship, and learning. Then we may "run out of years" but the fire of God's Spirit, of faith, hope, love, joy, peace, will continue to burn.

Deo gratias
Stuart Scott, March 2022

NOTE

I seek to be consistent in the use of upper case for "Church" when referring to denomination or the Church as an institution and in names of specific local churches. I also use upper case for "Minister", "Moderator", "Church Related Community Work Minister", "Synod" and the "Ministry of the Word and Sacraments". I use the lower case for "church" in referring generally to the local church, "elder", and more generic "ministry". I refer consistently to the "Ministry of *the* Word and Sacraments". This largely follows the forms used in the Basis of Union.[8] There is however a variety of use in the United Reformed Church.

Scripture quotations throughout the text are from the *New Revised Standard Version Bible*: Anglicized Edition, copyright © 1989, 1995 National Council of the Churches of Christ in the United States of America. Used by permission. All rights reserved worldwide.

---

8   United Reformed Church, n.d. The Manual. [Online] Available at: https://urc.org.uk/images/the_manual/A_The_Basis_of_union_23_01_2020.pdf [accessed 24th April 2020].

TWO

REFLECTION 1

MINISTRY IN ST JOHN'S UNITED REFORMED
CHURCH, STOURBRIDGE 2001–2016

BACKGROUND

In January 2001 I took up the part-time post of Lay Training Officer in the West Midlands Synod of the United Reformed Church. I had resigned from pastoral charge in two churches in Birmingham from 31st December 2000 and, with grant assistance from the Bible Society, I was continuing research into small churches for an MPhil at Manchester University.

In the early months of 2001 I was introduced to St John's United Reformed Church in Stourbridge. After meeting with the Church Council and others I was invited to "preach with a view" in May 2001. I received a call to serve as Minister there alongside the lay training role, a call which I accepted. In July 2001, at the end of the school term, I moved with my family from the Birmingham manse to Stourbridge. I was inducted into Ministry at St John's in September 2001.

The St John's Church building, opened in 1860, was formerly the Parish Church of St John the Evangelist. When the premises of the Congregational Church in Lower High Street, the successors of a congregation established in the town in 1662, needed significant repair work, the two congregations were persuaded to form a Local Ecumenical Partnership in the Anglican building. They worked together for over twenty-five years but prior to my arrival the partnership had been ended and in 1990 the premises were sold to the United Reformed Church. Shortly afterwards, the Diocese also sold the former church hall to Age Concern.

The pastorate profile indicated that at the time of my call there were fifty-three people on the church roll, thirty-four of whom were over sixty-five. Average attendance at worship was stated to be thirty-three. The profile stated, "We remain a loyal, loving congregation who steadfastly maintain regular witness and worship. However, our congregation is ageing and we are coming to recognise the difficulties in reaching out to others, especially young people and the middle aged." The profile went on to outline a vision for the short-term future:

"Over the next three years as a church we would like to:

- Have a clear vision of God's mission for St John's, to enable us to plan our church life and future accordingly
- Consider the use of the building for both worship, church-related weekday activities and other possible developments
- Actively encourage new church members initially in the twenty-five to forty-five-year-old range

- Continue the work already begun in restoring the church to a platform of sound finances, reducing the need for drawing on our investments for supporting our day-to-day expenditure
- Have a clear understanding of the ministry that we wish to offer to children and young people and how we can begin to improve on this
- Explore ecumenical links in Stourbridge town centre
- Grow in our understanding of the Bible
- Continue together and in small groups to build on the open and trusting relationships which are the basis of our activities."

I served as Minister of the Church for fifteen years, until October 2016, when I was offered the post of Training and Development Officer in the West Midlands Synod of the United Reformed Church on the condition that it was full-time. Reluctantly, and after considerable heart-searching, I accepted, bringing to an end a long, challenging and rewarding Ministry in Stourbridge. The town became home in a way that I had not experienced previously and when the church meeting agreed, only weeks after my leaving, that the church should close, I recognised a sense of loss and bereavement, not so much in relation to the building, but in the relationships, the activity and the adventure that were key to the life of the church.

The closing service took place at New Year in 2017. The loss of the leadership I had provided and a desperate need for major repairs to the chancel roof were suggested to have been the decisive factors, but one of the community partners, the

Black Country Radio Group, which had been broadcasting from a studio inside the building, had moved out months before to a purpose-built studio in neighbouring Brierley Hill. It was one of those involved in the management of the Radio Group who remarked to me, in the process of their move, and almost in passing, "We ran out of years".

The expression was perhaps appropriate then and seems increasingly appropriate now, both in relation to my own Ministry in the United Reformed Church and to a time of transition, challenge and change in the denomination. Personally, I am no more than a handful of years away from retirement. At this point I do not know what that means in precise detail, but it is almost certain that it will involve more limited activity. For the denomination there are discussions about the deployment of Ministers when many churches are small and struggling. There are tough decisions to be made, and urgent questions to be addressed. The journey ahead may be both challenging and rewarding, but the future of congregations increasing in age profile and experiencing significant numerical decline is uncertain, running out of years and facing closure.

In a very brief case study, written for my MPhil thesis, completed and submitted in 2006, I wrote this about St John's United Reformed Church, Stourbridge: *In a context of choice, this church can be seen as a ghetto for a small number of committed people. Within the congregation, there may be a variety of approaches to spirituality, as people attend church with a variety of needs, but worship follows a traditional pattern. At least on the surface, there appears to be little clear understanding of mission or readiness to engage in mission.*

The congregation's fundamental need and the dominant understanding of Ministry focus on Sunday worship. The goal of the church is probably expressed as survival, but further decline seems inevitable. The tone is very different from the high hopes of the 2000 pastorate profile, yet the doors were still open and there were exciting possibilities ahead.

In May 2004, a church meeting had explored its strengths, weaknesses, opportunities and threats. In November 2005 I wrote a paper: *St John's – our future.* In hindsight, this paper suggested too many options in relation to building, people and activity, but another church meeting agreed that it was no longer viable to continue in the Victorian listed building and further expenditure would be limited. A questionnaire was circulated to discern the way forward.

The responses to the questionnaire provided little clarity. A quinquennial survey on the building at the time indicated that the building was sound, but the roof required attention. Following discussion with the then District Pastoral Committee, it was agreed to propose to a church meeting that the church should close with a final service in January 2007 with transport provided to the Halesowen United Church, where I had also been serving as Minister since July 2005, when the scoping at St John's had been reduced from fifty per cent to twenty-five per cent. The St John's church meeting, however, agreed not to close in January but to explore community links and to make a decision on closure, perhaps at the end of June, at Easter 2007.

I wrote a further statement in January 2007 outlining the position. I stated: *The congregation of St John's are seeking to bring the building back to life and back into the community.*

This will not be possible without partners, and without possibly significant internal re-ordering of the church. It is hoped that the imaginative and creative development of the narthex,[9] thirty years ago, can be taken further for a new generation, while holding to the riches of the architectural heritage as far as possible. There are time constraints. Although important decisions must not be rushed and effective communication is paramount, it would be poor stewardship of resources for a small congregation to continue in this building if a viable future cannot be discerned. The congregation might continue to meet until reserves are expended, but would prefer not to do so. To this end, short-term, medium-term and long-term objectives are necessary.

The statement concluded: *The church is prepared to take the painful decision at Easter to move out of the present building and worship elsewhere.* In the event, front page headlines in the local press led to expressions of interest in using the building from a number of local groups. These included the Black Country Radio (at that point operating as 'Bridge Radio), Chawn Hill Church (an independent fellowship) for possible foodbank development, the Side by Side Theatre Company, working with adults with learning difficulties, and Age Concern, whose Stourbridge centre was in the neighbouring building, previously the church hall. There were conversations with key postholders in the community and charity sector and it also came to light that the Church of England had placed a restrictive covenant on

---

9   Using the funds from the sale of the Lower High Street site, the rear section of the nave was partitioned off to create an extended lobby area (technically the "narthex") and also provide for a kitchen and toilets.

the building when it had been declared redundant at the time of sale to the United Reformed Church.

A follow-up "position paper" was circulated in March 2007 and a church meeting in April agreed to commission a feasibility study and continue negotiation with 'Bridge Radio. In March 2009, a third "position paper" was circulated in the face of necessary and urgent repairs. £12,000 was needed for roof repairs and fundraising was agreed. However, a gas leak had revealed that the kitchen boiler also needed replacement with a further cost of £1,500. A working party, that had been exploring development since 2006, agreed steps of crisis management. The Side by Side Theatre Company, who had been using the nave for rehearsal, moved to the nearby Methodist Church for rehearsals but continued to use St John's for storage. Other activities, including the Black Country Foodbank, 'Bridge Radio broadcasting and Church activities such as worship, uniformed organizations, and Saturday coffee, continued to take place in the building.

The Church Council called a special church meeting to discuss the urgent repairs, the limited funds available and the limited resources of personnel. This statement was made; "All options appear to have been explored, the financial situation does not give us a great deal of time and closure may appear inevitable. Yet a way through the immediate crisis may be found." Options were put forward – closure, giving the users (the Radio Group, Side by Side and the foodbank) three months' notice, a special appeal, seeking interest-free loans, selling valuable items such as the eagle lectern at auction, engaging a fundraiser, and making funding applications. If closure was agreed, other decisions would need to follow such as continuing to meet elsewhere, conversations towards a sharing agreement, or dispersing. A number of factors had to be considered: the results of the feasibility study which had been undertaken in 2008; the process of discernment since February 2006; interest from a local entrepreneur in developing a low-carbon hub around St John's; results from funding applications including English Heritage; investment from the Radio Group; interest from Age Concern; the possibility of a third party taking over and developing the building while providing continuing hospitality; ecumenical possibilities involving a number of local churches.[10]

At this point, it was apparent that St John's was almost certainly running out of years and closure may have appeared inevitable. However, the fire continued to burn – literally, as a generous gift enabled the kitchen boiler to be replaced, and as a result of a successful funding application, urgent roof repairs were completed. The partnerships in place were becoming the focus of mission engagement and it was hoped to develop these and further partnerships with a view to long-term sustainability. There were no easy answers, no quick-fix solutions, no money trees but there were key factors continuing to take the church forward: a culture of welcome and a willingness to experiment; the strategic location of the building (next to the bus station, the railway station and ring road with easy access to the town centre);

---

10 Including the implications of the Church of England restrictive covenant on the St John's building, plans to develop New Road Methodist Church, discussions about the future location of Hanbury Hill Baptist Church, the provision of the Assisi Room at Our Lady and All Saints Roman Catholic Church, and the potential for partnership with the Chawn Hill Church.

partnerships in place, and ongoing conversations across churches and community groups; a building of significant historic and architectural interest. There was no denial of the vulnerability arising from the lack of finance and personnel, but closure was not inevitable.

In the years that followed there were further successful funding applications, though a rejection from English Heritage for grant assistance for the substantial work needed on the roof was in the course of time probably decisive. In addition to the partnership with the Radio Group and the foodbank, Stourbridge College Horticulture students, with a variety of learning difficulties, made significant progress in improving and developing the Church grounds and Gig Caritas, a local initiative through which musicians performed free of charge to raise funds for local charities, used St John's as the base for their activity. There were also other experiments in using the premises as display and performance space.

In spite of diminishing resources, the limitations of a nineteenth-century grade II listed building and years of neglect and lack of maintenance, St John's United Reformed Church responded to diverse needs and opportunities in witness and service to the end of 2016 and the building continued to have a future. However, it might also be seen as "too little, too late". Ultimately, St John's United Reformed Church was unable to take forward the vision for a sustainable future based on community partnerships, and the wider Church failed to understand this vision, as applications to the Synod Listed Buildings Advisory Committee met consistently with delay and demands for more information while an application to the Synod Mission Fund was rejected.

St John's United Reformed Church, Stourbridge "ran out of years". But, I ask, where does responsibility for the closure of St John's lie? According to the practice of the United Reformed Church, the decision to close was made by the church meeting. However, a number of factors contributed to that decision, which I now consider.

PEOPLE

By the time the Church closed, both membership and the average Sunday attendance were in single figures although on some special occasions, such as Remembrance Sunday and the Christingle service, the attendance was significantly higher. It was no longer possible to continue as a "loyal, loving congregation who steadfastly maintain regular witness and worship". It is perhaps particularly sad that, although suggestions were made for keeping the people together and encouragement was given to maintain the bonds of friendship and fellowship, the congregation dispersed, and only some to other churches in the town.

The decline in membership and in attendance was not particularly marked in comparison with other churches, and a few people had joined the church over the period. An ageing and declining congregation of Sunday worshippers however was unable to respond to particular challenges and opportunities. The treasurer remained in office after moving from the area and being unable to attend worship. There was insufficient leadership within the serving eldership and no possibility of others serving, and members of the congregation generally were reluctant to take responsibility and unable to grasp the vision that was being presented.

My role as the Minister might be seen as pivotal. I brought qualities, gifts and experience including sabbatical study and research into small churches (1998–2006) and into churches re-ordering for worship and witness (2008). Yet, as I was serving this church initially half-time and then from 2005 quarter-time, I could not carry alone the vision for sustainability and fruitfulness. It is no doubt significant that it was only weeks after I had moved on that the decision was made to close the church.

In the years before closure, partnerships with community groups had become increasingly vital to the vision for the church's future and sustainability, but at the point of closure there were few points of contact between the congregation and those groups. Some individuals outside the life of the worshipping community gave considerable time and energy to take the vision for the church forward and, as it was expressed in a strapline adopted, to put "life back into St John's and St John's back into the life of the community". There was some progress in that direction, but it did not prove possible to build sufficient bridges between the congregation and community groups before the years ran out.

It is not the case that all responsibility lies on one side. Some community groups and some of their participants did not identify with or engage fully with the life of the church. There were times when groups did not meet their financial commitments and groups had their own issues and agendas. More attention might have been given to strengthening the links and understanding the needs and aspirations of the different groups as partnerships developed. This would have been fruitful in the longer term and given the church greater control of its own future.

FINANCES

In the history of St John's, financial viability was a matter of concern over a very long period of time. The lack of reserves and the need to generate income were important influences on the church's life. At the time of closure at the end of 2016, the church in fact ran out of money, partly because income from the Radio Group had ceased.

Over my years as Minister at St John's, the treasurer carried the responsibility for the oversight and keeping of financial records and reported the financial situation regularly to meetings of the Church Council and church meetings. In later years he also copied statements to those with financial responsibility in the wider denomination.

It was regularly reported that funds would be exhausted by a specific date. For example, in November 2005, a document was circulated that indicated the weekly costs of running the church, the weekly income and the reserves available, and concluded that the church would run out of money in due course and perhaps within a very few years, while a quinquennial survey on the building would make further financial demands. It was therefore necessary either to increase income or reduce expenditure. Subsequently, in June 2008, expectations of income and expenditure led to projections that total assets at the end of 2009 would be £187.

Over this period, the treasurer moved from Stourbridge, initially to Much Wenlock and then to Oswestry. Ties of friendship and fellowship were maintained, but he no longer worshipped at the church or was in ongoing contact with the developing situation. Attempts were made to keep him informed and to involve him as far as possible, but the presentation of financial reports would normally be taken at the beginning of meetings and the treasurer would then leave. In consequence, when detailed projections were presented, they might be inaccurate. As circumstances changed, partnerships developed and funding applications were submitted, it was difficult to assess the actual situation at any particular time and the treasurer could be unaware of important income streams, grants or events.

As the Minister I was at times in the difficult position of having more accurate and encouraging information than was being presented. This led to some frustration and, with hindsight, this situation was allowed to continue for too long. In 2016 arrangements were made through one of the community groups to put the management of the church's finances into the hands of a local accountancy practice. This might have been done earlier but it had been previously felt that the situation would be resolved either through closure or a major redevelopment scheme. Alternatively, the necessary financial expertise might have been provided earlier either by another local church or from the Synod.

THE BUILDING

The American context is in many ways very different from that of the United Reformed Church in the United Kingdom, but can provide some pointers for collaboration and future direction. The *Alban Weekly* email on 16th February 2021 considered the issue of church buildings. Under the heading "Buildings – assets or albatrosses" it said, "One of the trends in congregational life we have been following for a while is how communities of faith relate to buildings. We've watched as some congregations deal with the issues that come with aging [sic] structures and deferred maintenance. Other congregations have chosen to share their physical spaces with social enterprises or nonprofits, both to help offset their costs and to expand their mission reach. Other congregations have sold their buildings entirely, choosing to rent alternative spaces for worship and community life. Now, of course, the pandemic has brought new questions about our relationship to buildings and shared spaces."[11]

The St John's, Stourbridge building is listed as Victorian modern Gothic and grade II by English Heritage. The architect was George E. Street, who went on to be responsible for a number of better-known buildings such as the Courts of Justice in the Strand. The listing presented both the greatest strength and the greatest weakness of the life of St John's Church. The congregation in general had no significant ties to this building. Most had either experienced the move of the Lower High Street Congregational Church into the Anglican building or had roots and previous allegiances and belonging elsewhere. As a result, the congregation was willing to move from the building if and when it became clear that the building could no longer fulfil its purpose, either because it was too

---

11 The Alban Institute provided education and advice to Protestant Church leaders in the USA through its publishing and consulting from the 1970s to its closure in 2014. Its education and consulting work continue through the Duke Divinity School's online publishing "Alban at Duke Divinity School" which, to quote the website (https://alban.org/), "helps leaders connect and learn from one another by sharing practical wisdom, stories of thriving congregations and transformational models of ministry". *Alban Weekly* is an email newsletter, which "offers stories of hope and practical wisdom on how to lead congregations today".

large for the congregation to sustain as a place of worship, or because it could not be adapted or refurbished owing to the constraints of the listing. A move out of the building might have been made earlier, but as the story unfolded needs were being met and partnerships were established due to the location and accessibility of the building. It could be argued that the architecture and the location comprised, in contemporary jargon, the "Unique Selling Point".

As has already been suggested, the demands of the fabric were themselves significant in bringing the church members to their decision to close the church. Although a great deal of work had been done towards refurbishment, redecoration, repairs and renewal, it was a hole in the roof that ultimately appeared insurmountable.

Substantial and successful funding applications had enabled survival but at the same time the listing made change and adaptation slow and difficult. Any change required the agreement of the Synod Property Committee on the recommendation of the Synod Listed Buildings Advisory Committee. From the church's perspective there appeared to be little understanding in these Committees of the precarious situation, and the system placed unnecessary obstacles in the way of innovation and experiment. On the other hand, users of the building who required and proposed change, for example, the Radio Group, did not always follow through with the information that was requested from them.

The 2008 feasibility study established potential for the building which was demonstrated by the variety of formal expressions of interest following the media coverage which first brought the church's situation to public attention. There was however no capacity to manage or maintain the premises, so the potential remained largely unfulfilled.

The church was nevertheless able, through initial contact with Gig Caritas, to participate in a major research project into the potential of community design for historic places of worship under the title "Empowering Design Practices". This project presented its final report, which featured St John's,[12] in early 2020. The initial meeting with the researchers appeared positive, encouraging and promising and the project team provided resources and ran a workshop at St John's. There was limited response or participation from the congregation or the community groups using the building, or recognition in the wider United Reformed Church of the potential of the research project in relation to St John's' future.[13]

There is of course a wider narrative and debate about buildings, and about listed buildings and historic places of worship specifically, that is not directly relevant here. Several months after the closure of St John's as a United Reformed Church, the Side by Side Theatre Group raised funds, bought

---

12 "St John's United Reformed Church (Stourbridge): A 19th-century Church by Victorian architect G. E. Street, it was acquired by the United Reformed Church in 1990. In recent years, the Church hosted tenants Black Country Radio and users including Rainbows and Guides, a foodbank and many concerts and exhibitions. We began working with the congregation at St John's in 2016 to support them in exploring how the building could better cater for these diverse uses. However, in 2017, with a growing list of repairs and limited resources with which to tackle them, St John's made the difficult decision to close their Church and the congregation have now moved elsewhere." https://www.empoweringdesign.net/longitudinal-projects.html [accessed 24th April 2020].

13 https://www.empoweringdesign.net/ [accessed 24th April 2020].

the site, invested significantly in the repair and adaptation of St John's and continue to develop it as rehearsal and performance space, "SideSpace at St John's".[14] As they develop the building it is likely that other community groups will also be accommodated.

CONCLUSION

Rachel Mann writes, *Being creatures limited by time, it is unsurprising that we are haunted by the past – one's own and of one's community. Time ensures that living well entails loss.*[15] It is always the case that we "run out of years"; there is always an end. God brings life into being and nurtures and nourishes it. In response we seek fruitfulness and faithfulness, but when God brings life to an end, we give thanks and let go, while holding on to precious memories, and committing ourselves to each other as far as is possible, and to the future, whatever it may hold.

There are a number of issues which need to be addressed in relation to struggling and vulnerable churches and decisions to close. A strategic approach is crucial which goes beyond bank balances and membership rolls and gives attention to leadership development, discovering vocation, discerning gifts and exploring creative approaches to mission and ministry. A process of discernment is needed which balances subjectivity and objectivity, deals with endings and the associated grief with pastoral sensitivity, and provides effective support and clear guidance through difficult processes of transition and change.

---

14   http://thesidespace.org/ [accessed 24th April 2020].
15   Mann, R. 2017 p.81.

We always run out of years, at some point, in God's good time and in God's good and loving purpose. But there is also always a bigger picture. It's not about us, as individuals, or as churches, as communities of people seeking to respond in faith and love and follow in the way of Jesus Christ as Saviour and as Lord. There is loss but there is grace and hope, and even resurrection. We see only a small part of the picture; we share only a small part of the story.

From my experience as Minister in Stourbridge and previously I suggest that the local church should be given as much freedom as possible to respond to its own context and to embrace experiment and change. It will need support, guidance and encouragement from the wider denomination to develop its own resources of people, buildings, and finance. In such contexts the leadership, nurture, teaching and sustenance provided by the Ministry of the Word and Sacraments is key. Specifically, if St John's had been given the support it requested and its Ministry not been reduced at a crucial time, the potential for the continued use of the building in worship and witness, discipleship and mission might have been fulfilled.

QUESTIONS FOR DISCUSSION

- What are the key resources – spiritual, theological, social, financial or other – for the viability and sustainability of Christian congregations and local churches? Is there a "hierarchy of needs" that might be applied?
- Where and how might a strategic approach to the location of local churches and the deployment of Ministry be effectively and sensitively developed?
- What are the implications of historic and potentially iconic buildings for mission and Ministry, and specifically for worship and community life? Are they inevitably millstones and no longer appropriate for worship and mission? How might creative approaches open fresh opportunities?
- What is the impact of history and culture in a particular setting on Christian identity and witness?

St John's United Reformed Church March 2011

St John's Church nave and chancel
facing east June 2010

St John's Remembrance
Sunday 2014
Photo John Syed (reproduced
with permission)

St John's Church nave and narthex
facing west June 2010

Narthex and radio studio in St
John's October 2016
Photo Paul Collins (reproduced
with permission)

Radio studio at St John's
October 2016
Photo Paul Collins (reproduced with
permission)

THREE

REFLECTION 2

WHAT ARE MINISTERS FOR?

BACKGROUND: WHAT IS THE SPIRIT SAYING TO THE CHURCHES?

From 2014 to 2016 the Faith and Order Committee of the United Reformed Church led discussion and consultation across the Church with the title "What is the Spirit saying to the Churches?".[16] An edited version of material presented to the 2016 General Assembly remains available online. The website declares, "Our Church has a calling to live, a task to fulfil, a great God to serve, and grace sufficient for the journey ahead. We hope that people will find this message refreshingly positive. In some Churches it may give resource material for preaching or discussion. We

---

16   United Reformed Church 2014 and 2016.

commend it to you, and commend you to God's guidance, wisdom and love."[17]

In the face of a twofold reality undergirding the discussion, numerical decline and "functional atheism", the loss of confidence in God, trust in the significance of the Holy Trinity was emphasised "in giving life to and shaping the Church, and not only this, but offering, as has been done over many centuries, life and freedom for the world". The focus is on congregational life rather than ministry or mission.

Five possible scenarios for the future of the denomination were presented. There was no support in ensuing discussion for holding the status quo, but concern was expressed about losing identity. There was resistance to major structural reorganisation, but it was recognised that variety in patterns of church life was already the reality.

There was a desire to refocus on spirituality, theological reflection and practical local initiatives. Some diverse challenges were recognised: cultural shift, the role of reason and experience, the nature of authority, relationship to institutions, approaches to scripture, the tension between personal autonomy and community, and the place of structures in the life of the Church. Movement was perceived as being away from a providential understanding of God, acting in history and providing for God's people in various ways, to causality, God as a cause of events and experience but not acting directly. There was movement too away from institution to self with

---

17 https://urc.org.uk/urc-resources/faith-and-order/2572-what-is-the-spirit-saying-to-the-Churches.html [accessed 22nd April 2020].

a focus on self-expression and self-realisation rather than religious institutions, rules or mutual belonging.

Hard work and commitment were required to effect change in congregational life but in the light of glimpses of eternity. Two dilemmas might hold the Church back: a sense of despair and negativity and a focus on details and activities rather than the bigger picture. Opportunities, the report suggested, need to be given to name fears and anxieties but to focus on the joy of life in Christ, the energising of the Holy Spirit and the vision that God holds out. Strategy emerges from vision and management develops from strategy.

The report suggested two further scenarios might have been presented: the death of the United Reformed Church or an over-optimistic and unrealistic scenario of growth. On the first there was a deliberate choice not to offer a strategy for the closing of churches, on the basis that the work of the Spirit is focused on growth and fruitfulness. There was also a conscious decision not to present the second alternative.

The identity of the United Reformed Church was considered, its values and passions and the ways in which the Holy Spirit is discovered. There would be a separate paper on conciliarity and, following further work, a paper on eldership, but there is detailed discussion on being "reformed" and "united". Congregations were encouraged to revisit the Basis of Union and the Statement of the Nature, Faith and Order of the United Reformed Church.

The report maintained a positive and encouraging tone, and provided a basis for discussion that was realistic about the state of the Church while also confirming the nature of God. The future of the Church was affirmed, but it stated that there are no easy answers or quick fixes. I suggest that denominational initiatives and programmes can appear disconnected and reactive, and proactive and strategic planning are needed for the longer term, while recognising that planning is always contingent and provisional.

The report suggested a need for openness rather than a specific plan, structure or programme, but did not include or promote significant discussion of Ministry. It described this practical issue: "Revisit the nature of ministry and the relation between lay and ordained ministry, particularly in the light of deployment. This work is in progress." This challenge was made instead to congregations: "The United Reformed Church affirms that the renewal of congregational life is key to the renewal of the Church. Without congregations, there is no Church. This is not about a 'one size fits all' idea of a congregation – congregations vary enormously; it is about the way in which people are valued and held together. We affirm that in the body of Christ, congregations are held together with one another, sharing insights and support for mutual enrichment. The United Reformed Church has a particular contribution to make about the way in which authority is held within and between congregations." I suggest authority is increasingly a key issue as churches decline numerically and resources diminish.

There was a specific challenge to congregations and to the wider Church to hold together unity and diversity, to chart the territory of order and consistency on the one hand and flexibility on the other. The report continued,

"There are important questions about the way our wider structures enable mutual enrichment. But, prior to these are the questions around whether our congregations feel on fire with a Gospel that is for all people and are able to communicate this fire with the communities in which we are placed. This passion arises out of people's rootedness in God and their openness to the Holy Spirit through prayer, worship and the reading of Scripture, those aspects of our shared life which have sustained God's people over the generations". The passion for the gospel in the churches is, I suggest, another key issue and Ministry of the Word and Sacraments has a vital role in engendering this response, equipping and inspiring the people of God gathered for worship for their lives of witness, discipleship and service.

The Faith and Order Committee offered six affirmations in responding to the report, including elements of celebration, potential and challenge. The fourth affirms the value of the local church: "God in Trinity draws people into a relationship of love... We affirm the value of the local Church as the place in which God's love is known and lived out. The URC celebrates the whole people of God, each one, young and old, with his or her own gifting from the Spirit, each one given voice by the Holy Spirit." In my view, attention needs to be given to how those gifts are used, how and whether the voices are heard.

The Faith and Order Committee also suggested ways in which the moving of the Holy Spirit is evident in the life of the denomination, all of which have some reference to Ministry: the ordination of women, ministry among and with children and young people, the development of team and Non-stipendiary Ministry, the affirmation and consolidation of the role of elders, work on the margins through the Church Related Community Work (CRCW) programme, and racial justice and multi-cultural ministry. It was recognised these were grounds for celebration, but there are also challenges: the Ministries Committee were working on a variety of issues and pressures faced by Ministers and congregations arising from the deployment of Ministers, who were spread increasingly thinly across churches. With challenges come new possibilities, and the Committee pointed to the possibility of consideration of the World Council of Churches report "The Church: Towards a common vision", on the issues of ministry and authority in relation to unity.

The Committee affirmed elders as "a particular gift to the United Reformed Church, set aside in each congregation for spiritual leadership and pastoral care", and Ministers of the Word and Sacraments as "entrusted with oversight and inspiration of each congregation" with "a particular role in leadership". Elders and Ministers share together in offering leadership to the local church, but others too offer specific gifts, particularly in leading worship. The United Reformed Church recognises, values and is increasingly dependent on lay preachers. Training is not required for this ministry, but financial and other support are provided. Church order does require ordination for presidency at the Sacraments. At the formation of the United Reformed Church in 1972 the Basis of Union provided for lay presidency in case of "pastoral necessity". A consequence of the introduction of "authorised eldership"[18] has been a greater degree of consistency of practice.

PRIORITIES FOR MINISTRY

I suggest that the understanding of Ministry has key implications for congregational life and health. "What is the Spirit saying…" recognised challenges to personal and community life. It is important too to consider priorities for ministry, the roles and functions of those called to exercise formal ministries, particularly ordination to Ministry of the Word and Sacraments. There are too many assumptions and too much is taken for granted and some basic questions need to be addressed: How is Ministry of the Word and Sacraments understood? What should Ministers do? What are Ministers for? How do formal ministries contribute to the renewal of congregational life? I argue that there might be no renewal of congregational life without renewal through the Word and Sacraments.

According to the Basis of Union, the Minister brings the wider Church to the local. That is to say, the Minister represents catholicity and apostolicity to the local church. Ordained Ministry of the Word and Sacraments provides leadership to the church and this leadership is exercised in four roles – leading worship, presiding at the Sacraments, pastoral care and leading the church in its engagement with the world in discipleship, witness and service. The

---

18 https://urc.org.uk/images/General-Assemblies/Assembly2016/ assembly_reports_16.pdf pp.90-107 and https:/./urc.org.uk/images/ General-Assemblies/Assembly2016/RECORD-2016w.pdf p.33 [accessed 18th March 2021].

Baptism, Eucharist and Ministry paper of the World Council of Churches said, "The chief responsibility of the ordained ministry is to assemble and build up the body of Christ by proclaiming and teaching the Word of God, by celebrating the Sacraments, and by guiding the life of the community in its worship, its mission and its caring ministry". This ministry is "bound to the faithful in interdependence and reciprocity".[19]

It is clear that there is no single pattern for leadership in the Church in the New Testament. A key passage is Ephesians 4.11-16: *The gifts he gave were that some would be apostles, some prophets, some evangelists, some pastors and teachers, to equip the saints for the work of ministry, for building up the body of Christ, until all of us come to the unity of the faith and of the knowledge of the Son of God, to maturity, to the measure of the full stature of Christ. We must no longer be children, tossed to and fro and blown about by every wind of doctrine, by people's trickery, by their craftiness in deceitful scheming. But speaking the truth in love, we must grow up in every way into him who is the head, into Christ, from whom the whole body, joined and knitted together by every ligament with which it is equipped, as each part is working properly, promotes the body's growth in building itself up in love* (Ephesians 4:11-16, *NRSV*).

THE NATURE AND PURPOSE OF THE CHURCH
The United Reformed Church aspires to be a learning Church, where all are called and commit themselves to lifelong learning, developing understanding and discipleship. Roles

---

19 Willimon, W. H. (ed.) 2002 p.35.

and responsibilities may need to be open to development and change and the United Reformed Church declares itself open to change ("*semper reformanda*" in the phrase popularised by Karl Barth) but individuals develop and change too. The drama of human life takes place within the greater drama of the divine life.[20] We "run out of years" as part of human experience but the divine story continues. The leadership provided through the Ministry of the Word and Sacraments is instrumental in the human story sharing the divine story, encouraging spiritual growth to maturity of individuals and congregations.

The Reformed tradition affirms the priesthood of all believers. There is no radical distinction between clergy and laity but it is not the case that anyone can do anything. Any specific task might be undertaken by any individual, whether ordained or not, but ordination to the Ministry of the Word and Sacraments recognises particular gifts, capacities, aptitudes, skills and insights in an individual who is then set apart. The Church, as Calvin says, can be seen where the Word of God is duly preached and heard and the Sacraments are administered according to Christ's institution. On these grounds there has to be the Word and Sacraments for the Church to be seen to be the Church.[21] This has important implications for the Ministry of the Word and Sacraments, and for discussions and decisions on the deployment

---

20 Fiddes, P. 2000 p.184.

21 Calvin, J. 1960 IV I 9. Calvin says that where this occurs we can be sure that a Church of God exists. But the Word and Sacraments do not constitute the Church. Instead it is God's grace that constitutes the Church. I am grateful to Robert Pope for this point.

of Ministers, and makes attention to vocation and the affirmation of those called to serve in this way essential.

Ecclesiology, the understanding of the nature and purpose of the Church, might determine the pattern of ministry. Any pattern of ministry however has personal, collegial and communal aspects.[22] The local church might be mission-shaped, but there are implications for Ministry of the Word and Sacraments. Ordained Ministry equips and sustains the Church for participation in God's mission alongside proclaiming the gospel and celebrating the Sacraments. That participation is a local expression, and determined by context.

"What is the Spirit saying to the Churches?" reminded the United Reformed Church of the significance of being united and reformed but perhaps more importantly of the necessity of "rootedness in God" and "openness to the Holy Spirit". Ministry of the Word and Sacraments contributes directly to these essential characteristics.

The realism the report sought is also against the background of the United Reformed Church as a denomination of small churches. In 1972, when the United Reformed Church came into being with the union of congregations of the Congregational Church in England and Wales and the Presbyterian Church of England, there was an aspiration to have Ministry available to all Churches.[23] In contrast to such aspirations and expectations, the shape

---

22 Willimon, W. H. (ed.) 2002.

23 Basis of Union paragraph 25 (with thanks to Robert Pope for this reference).

of ministry must now fit a Church of many small groups.[24] Structures established in 1972 might have been appropriate for churches of the Presbyterian tradition. Congregational Churches at that time were generally smaller, with a greater dependence on local leadership. This presents an undoubted challenge at this time, when a lack of local leadership and an overdependence on ordained Ministry is evident.

David Peel notes *The URC by and large is a collection of small churches. It is sometimes difficult for the members of the minority of larger, usually suburban churches to realize this, or to avoid the rather fallacious inference that a small church is a weak church. Some are weak, but so are some of our larger congregations.*[25] Models of mission however tend to assume

---

24 In 1983 the Baptist Union Department of Ministry published the report of Working Group on the Care of Small Churches with the title "Half the Denomination". A concluding section, "Towards a new model of leadership", proposed a combination of "corporate leadership" and "individual leadership". "Corporate leadership" would be provided by pastoral teams with several types of people and gifts. It was suggested this would enable current gifts to be used more effectively if each lay preacher was assigned to a limited number of Churches or even a single Church. "Individual leadership" would include the provision of more "lay pastors" with responsibility for leadership of small Churches but not carrying alone the responsibility of preaching, pastoral care and administration. Recommendations were made for their support, training and for recognition. Reference was also made to "Supplementary Ministries", and the report's conclusion encourages Baptists to move beyond their traditional individualism to explore partnership and collaboration between Churches. There was little or no follow-up to this report among Baptist Churches but it foreshadows much of the development of Ministry – team ministries, joint pastorates and Non-stipendiary Ministry – in the United Reformed Church that will be considered in this and following reflections.

25 Peel, D. 2003 p.91.

that bigger is better. I suggest that growth and renewal might look towards the proliferation of small and locally focused groups, built up through worship and prayer and in this way equipped to live out the gospel faith in rooted relationships. Attention is needed to appropriate patterns and styles of ministry for each context and the implications for discerning call, and for training requirements of the consequent diversity.

Avery Dulles offered a number of models of the Church: institution, mystical communion, sacrament, herald, servant, and, in a more recent addition to the book, community of disciples.[26] A balanced theology, he concludes, must incorporate the major affirmations of each. He argued that models can have great value in helping people to get beyond the limitations of their own particular outlook and to enter into fruitful conversation with others. He saw conversation as essential for the future of ecumenical partnership, as the way of getting beyond the impasses of that time. Conversation across and beyond denominational boundaries might be a way forward for the United Reformed Church, as it seeks to respond to current challenges and opportunities, and to explore diversity with consistency within the institution. Some elements of "normal" practice might be established, with freedom to experiment and to work outside those norms as the Spirit leads.

Lesslie Newbigin described the Church as the sign, instrument and foretaste of the kingdom of God.[27] The kingdom, the rule and reign of God, frames the identity and purpose of

---

26 Dulles, A. 1978.

27 Newbigin, L. 1978, revised 1995.

the whole Church. This has implications for its interior life as well as its participation in God's mission, the "*missio dei*".

Mission has become the driving force for much local church and wider Church activity and the focus for the provision of resources, but this may fail to balance all the dimensions of Christian faith and life – towards God, towards the self, towards fellowship in the church as the body of Christ, as well as towards the community, and towards the environment. Mission can become activity for its own sake rather than the recognition of God's prior presence and action. The work of the Holy Spirit in renewal must underpin all aspects of Christian life – worship and preaching, discipleship, witness and service, through pastoral care and in other ways, life in the Church and in the world.

Discipleship is "24/7" and life in the Spirit is the foundation for participation in the "*missio dei*", which requires vulnerability and openness, the ability to listen and to respond to need, and wisdom and discernment in responding to the wind of the Spirit. People do not come to Christian faith out of nowhere but in response to the leading and guiding of God's Spirit. Ministry of the Word and Sacraments might be an agent of renewal as the journey of growing faith and understanding is shared. The Church is the "sign, instrument and foretaste of the kingdom of God" with good news to be proclaimed in word and action. Faith must be lived out and such living out is resourced through the Word and Sacraments.

In some contexts the Minister might be the driving force behind activity and in others equip the church for its evangelistic task. The formation of new ecclesial communities and Fresh Expressions[28] will also have an impact on Ministry and deployment, although at present the overall effect is not clear. Further, statistical data for the denomination continues to be requested and presented on the basis of Sunday worship. There is also clarity in the Church's expectations of ordained Ministry.

MARKS OF MINISTRY

In May 2019, the Mission Council of the United Reformed Church adopted this description "of what the Church can reasonably expect of people who are called to the Ministry of the Word and Sacraments" although "it was acknowledged that what this will look like in each Minister will vary depending on the context, the individual, and the specific Ministry to which they are called".

- **A faithful disciple of Jesus Christ:** caught up in the joy and wonder of God's will and work; seeking always to live a holy life in public and in private; sustained by their own rhythm of prayer, Bible reading and worship so that they might model and encourage such lifelong patterns in others with integrity; open to learning discipleship from others.
- **A person of integrity and resilience:** self-aware and committed to their own lifelong learning (especially through the URC's provision for Ministers); aware of their own limitations and thus willing to seek support; ready to deal with situations of conflict;

28 https://freshexpressions.org.uk/ [accessed 24th April 2020].

balancing ministry's joys and pains with the fostering of right relationships with family and friends.

- **A contextual theologian:** delighting in Scripture, rooted in the Reformed tradition, able to communicate their own faith and its implications within and beyond congregations; encouraging others to discover how these rich resources inspire and sustain faithfulness.

- **A worship leader and preacher:** able to craft and lead worship that shows appreciation for the Sacraments and the resources of many traditions and styles yet unafraid to create and advocate new forms as appropriate; passionate and effective in breaking open God's Word in preaching; ready and able to foster skills, techniques and experience in others so that they might lead worship and preach well.

- **A pastor:** sharing with others, especially elders, in sustaining care; making time to walk in love alongside people; rejoicing and grieving with others through listening deeply and offering prayerful support; wise in knowing their limits and boundaries when more specialized help is needed; reliably dealing with issues of safeguarding and confidentiality.

- **A leader and collaborator:** identifying, developing, and enabling leadership in others, particularly elders; capable of working in, and leading, teams through collaborative and shared leadership; aware of their own leadership style and open to learning with and from others, when necessary acknowledging their own mistakes and seeking restoration; committed and equipped to building up others in faith and witness so that the gifts and callings of all might flourish; demonstrating love for God's people.

- **A missionary and evangelist:** passionate about and active in sharing the love of God for the world; alive to the significance of contexts and cultures in shaping mission and creative in discovering missional opportunities; empowering and equipping God's people in mission to share the Gospel and live God's Kingdom of justice and peace to the full.
- **A public figure:** reliable and effective in representing the Church in ecumenical, community and wider settings; committed to and equipped in speaking truth to power and challenging injustice and marginalisation wherever they may be found.
- **A communicator:** who uses written, spoken and other modes with clarity and grace to share faith and build up relationships and communities; helping others to find their voice.
- **A committed participant in the councils of the Church:** responsive to God's call as gift and blessing to be lived out within the discipline and accountability of the denomination which trains, ordains and inducts them and the pastorates and ministries within which they serve.
- **A reformer:** wise in the dynamics and challenges of change; bold yet humble in helping individuals and congregations to discern and respond to the leading of the Holy Spirit as new chapters open in the life of the Church and others close.

In adopting this paper, the Mission Council resolved to "encourage the Ministries Committee, Education and Learning Committee, Resource Centres for Learning, and relevant Committees in all the Synods to use this description as the basis for consistency in expectations and reporting in relation to the Ministry of the Word and Sacraments". The aim of consistency is of course to be applauded but it might be seen to present the Minister of the Word and Sacraments as solely responsible for the renewal of the local church. I do not suggest that the statement places excessive demands on the Minister of the Word and Sacraments, but it must be read in the light of the call to every Christian disciple to "walk the way" and "live the life of Jesus today". If the Church is to be "the sign, instrument and foretaste of the kingdom of God" it is incumbent on each individual Christian to accept the demands and necessity of participation and to take seriously their own responsibility in worship, witness and service. Christian life is the life of a disciple and follower of Jesus Christ, life with God but also life in God, living each day in the light of God's presence and action, in the power and promise of the indwelling of the Holy Spirit.

THE RENEWAL OF THE LOCAL CHURCH

"What is the Spirit saying to the Churches?", and the Faith and Order Committee's response, emphasised the priority of the renewal of local churches. Renewal is neither the sole task nor the sole responsibility of the Minister of the Word and Sacraments. P. T. Forsyth argued in relation to the use of the Bible, *The real strength of a church is not the amount of its work but the quality of its fruit*. It is *tempting to look to*

Ministers to turn things round, he continued, but this *must be resisted unless Ministers point us to what is truly required, a renewed acquaintance with the gospel.*[29]

In exploring the Ministry and mission of small churches twenty years ago, I examined four different ways of being a small church. These were the declining church, the church plant, the cell church and the inherently small church. I suggested that variety and diversity were vital for local churches to respond to their local context. "What is the Spirit saying to the Churches?" suggested the response of the United Reformed Church as a denomination too often focused on the viability and sustainability of a particular form, and particular structures and activities. Viability and sustainability in such narrow terms may not be the key issue. I suggest we need to travel light, to be fleet of foot, and to be creative and imaginative. We need to be able to take risks, to embrace adventure, and to move and change and adapt as the world changes around us.

We might do old things in new ways and new things in new ways. Some practices might be brought to an end but there will be new possibilities and potential. We have known a particular pattern and have prepared Ministers of the Word and Sacraments in a variety of ways but predominantly to work within an established pattern. The future pattern will be different and Ministers may therefore need to acquire different gifts, aptitudes, skills, insights and capacities. Yet theological and ecclesiastical integrity must be maintained – the Church will still need the Word and Sacraments.

---

29 Peel, D. 2007 p.268.

Too much time and energy is possibly expended and a disproportionate financial investment is made on maintaining the status quo, keeping things as they are. There is room for experiment, but in general very limited resources are available for initiatives that take significant risks or need longer-term investment towards sustainability. The declared aim is to be a learning Church and there is a commitment to lifelong learning, but the investment in training for Ministers should then be mirrored in training for congregations and churches and for elders called and elected to lead them.

If learning is to be encouraged, more leadership is needed, which requires recognition, resourcing and support. If the development of a learning Church is to be more than aspirational, the commitment to lifelong learning and discipleship must be a characteristic of ordained Ministers, modelled and passed on to congregations and lay leadership. The training of Ministers of the Word and Sacraments should equip them to be a theological resource and to train elders for their roles and responsibilities, building up the whole Church as the people of God, as disciples and lifelong learners.

In *Ministry for Mission*, David Peel invited the Church to *Look death in the eye*.[30] He argued further that the *Holy Spirit is oblivious to strategic planning for opening and closing churches. There is scope for rationalization. Members are no guide to viability and faithfulness matters more than size. The seeds of demise are seen in complacency while small communities can be effective. Enablement, empowerment,*

---

30 Peel, D. 2003 p.73.

encouragement can be key.[31] Radical change may need to be negotiated but it is often not change itself that is particularly difficult or stressful but the processes of change, which are likely to be neither quick nor simple, as they require letting go of cherished practices and the experience of grief and loss. Yet the faith we hold is rooted in resurrection. There are endings but also new beginnings. The challenge to the wider Church may be to enable and resource both.

The management of change requires attention and change raises particular issues in an institution where decisions are made and authority is exercised from the bottom up. The centralisation of authority and decision-making will be fiercely (and rightly) resisted. The aspirations of Synod and denominational officers, and of the denomination's wider Councils and Committees, need to be accepted and owned by local churches. Otherwise, there is no forward movement and the likelihood of opposition. If local churches are to accept significant change vision needs to be discerned at all levels of the Church and processes must be carefully managed.

There is a particular issue around the closure of local churches – where, and by whom, are decisions about viability made? I suggest attention should be given to at least ensuring some continuity of worship and witness for the local church, supporting the exploration of new possibilities and potential while bringing to a dignified end forms of activity that are discerned to be no longer viable or sustainable.

Time and place are significant. It is part of human experience that we run out of years. Yet even when we run

---

31 Peel, D. 2003 p.90.

out of years, it is not the end of the story which begins and ends with God. Exploring "the Living God and the threat of death" in developing a pastoral doctrine of the Trinity, Fiddes writes: *death provides a boundary that makes sense of life. Any story needs an end as well as a beginning and a middle, and the conclusion of death makes human life into a meaningful story rather than just a succession of incidents or a 'tale/told by an idiot, full of sound and fury/signifying nothing'. Novels and plays bear abundant witness to the tragedy of those who cannot face death and find they have no story.* [32]

Fiddes continues, *We discover about death from experiencing the running out of time. We experience death as the final deadline, the last boundary in the face of which we feel time passing*[33] but *in the face of death we have to trust God to overcome an energy to life and to re-create, to make again from nothingness. We may trust God that new creation will fulfil all our hopes, but it is a real future that we cannot predict or map, not just an extension of the present; we step out into the unknown.*[34]

In the face of death, we proclaim resurrection and the promise of new life. There is always hope, the potential for renewal. We need to be in the right place at the right time, to trust in the renewal that God brings in the gift and power of the Holy Spirit. We need continually to learn and reflect in the light of the scriptures and in God's continuing provision for human need. The local church, as the sign, instrument and foretaste of the kingdom of God requires the leadership

32 Fiddes, P. 2000 p.237.
33 Fiddes, P. 2000 p.238.
34 Fiddes, P. 2000 p.246.

and resourcing through the Word and Sacraments that is offered through ordained Ministry.

EXPECTATIONS AND ESSENTIAL TASKS

Churches look to the Minister, and especially a Minister new in post, either to bring the change and new energy they seek or to reinforce their current practice in continuing to offer nurture and support. The Minister, guided by the Holy Spirit, receives and accepts a call to a particular place but cannot meet the range of expectations that are likely to be present in congregations and communities. The consequence can be disappointment and frustration on all sides – for the Minister, for the local church and the wider Church, and for the community where the local church offers its worship, witness and service. Changes might be made in the training and preparation of Ministers of the Word and Sacraments, to equip them to be resilient and to develop their capacity to serve for the long term.

There is however an essential and urgent educational task in the churches and the question arises – who is to undertake that task? There is no system in place which offers consistency across the thirteen Synods of the United Reformed Church. Some Synods appoint a Training and Development Officer or similar to develop and share (rather than undertake) the responsibility of promoting a "learning Church". These posts are not all filled by Ministers of the Word and Sacraments. In any case, the number of appointments is likely to decrease as the number of Ministers available to the denomination decreases. I suggest that the educational task is that of every Minister, to be a theological resource, a practical theologian.

It is a role that might be taken for granted, alongside knowledge of the Bible. As Hauerwas and Willimon suggest, *theology, to be Christian, is by definition practical.*[35] Theology needs to be applied and biblical knowledge needs to make a difference in the life of every believer.

In an age of "sound-bites" and diminishing attention spans, the Church needs to rediscover the Bible to challenge, equip, strengthen and develop the spiritual life of the individual disciple and follower of Jesus and the life of the local church. This is the task of the Minister of the Word and Sacraments. P. T. Forsyth emphasised preaching and teaching with high theological demands. The primary functions of Ministers are preaching and prayer, pastoral work, priest and prophet (also requiring prayer) and social and philanthropic functions outside the Church but he described a decline in standards of leadership and urged the religious public to cease to degrade the Ministry and to make greater demands to rediscover its roots in the gospel. This requires an educated rather than simply trained Ministry.[36] Daniel Jenkins similarly describes the role of the Minister as preacher, theologian and witness and Peel encourages an *extensive and costly commitment to theological education.*[37]

Brueggemann offers another view of the preacher in *Finally Comes the Poet.* He says ... *I want to consider preaching as a poetic construal of an alternative world. The purpose of such preaching is to cherish the truth, to open the truth from*

---

35 Willimon, W. H. (ed.) 2002 p.240.

36 Peel, D. 2007.

37 Peel, D. 2007 p.240.

*its pervasive reductionism in our society, to break the fearful
rationality that keeps the news from being new.*[38]

In February 2021, on the morning after the inauguration
of President Joe Biden and Vice-President Kamala Harris
in the United States, Nick Baines, the Anglican Bishop
of Leeds, presented "Thought for the Day" on Radio 4's
Today programme. He commented that the inauguration
ceremony had been "pregnant with resonant language" and
said, "The thing about yesterday was that, whether spoken or
accompanied by music, words have the power to transcend
mere pragmatism – policies and how to enact them in
legislation, for instance; they inspire the imagination. This
is language that resonates, that is spacious, that lifts our eyes
and hearts to perceive an experience that might hitherto have
eluded us." The poetry in particular, he suggested,[39] "clears a
way for hope" and, he concluded, "Surely it's the poets who
penetrate the jungle of defended argument and debate. For
the poet uses words to shine light from a different angle,
surprising the imagination, subverting expectation, and
opening our eyes to a new possibility. In silent vigil for those
who have died of Covid [sic], Joe Biden said: 'To heal, we must
remember.'"[40] Nick Spencer also describes being captivated
on his journey to faith by poets and poems that wrestled with
the pain of faith and doubt.[41] Further, in his reflection on

38 https://www.amazon.com/Finally-Comes-Poet-Walter-Brueggemann
    /dp/0800623940 [accessed 16th March 2021].

39 Nick Baines was referring to the poetry of Amanda Gorman, read by
    the poet herself at the inauguration

40 https://nickbaines.wordpress.com/tag/thought-for-the-day/ [accessed
    15th February 2021].

41 Spencer, N. in Holland, T. (ed.) 2020 p.77

George Herbert's "The Quidditie" Oakley comments: *As he uses poetry... it becomes a place of sacred encounter. He knows that he is with God when with poetry. The distillation, the freshness and surprise of poetry, its invitation into the deeper currents, all make it holy ground. Poetry explores the immense intimacies and the intimate immensities of life and the world and it is in these that God's presence burns like a scorching and defrosting fire.*[42]

There is also, I suggest, frequent collusion between "pulpit" and "pew" which maintains the status quo and keeps things as they are and the institution is inherently resistant to change. Against this background, healthy and life-giving relationships of mutual care and support will be one key to embracing change and fuller effectiveness in witness and service.

A sense of belonging is vital to identity, meaning and purpose. Grace Davie explored (and more recently revised) the connection between believing and belonging and the consequences for behaviour. Contrary to perceptions of standards of acceptable faith and behaviour in which only those who could demonstrate right belief and right behaviour would be allowed to belong, Davie provides evidence that developing a sense of belonging precedes belief, and belief and belonging then shape behaviour, values, attitudes and ethics.[43] A paradigm shift is needed in church life, away from the predominance of passive consumerism and dependency towards active engagement, participation, belonging and interdependency.

---

42 Oakley, M. 2019 pp.42-43.
43 Davie, G. 1994 and 2015.

This might be achieved through the formation of small groups and the encouragement of reflective practice.

Healthy and life-giving relationships are developed through nurture and pastoral care. Pastoral care is another primary task of the ordained Minister. Henri Nouwen describes this task as *loving because loved, giving because receiving and free because set free.*[44] It is central in the local church's expectations but an expectation that is increasingly difficult to meet, since it requires the investment of considerable time to do well and time is limited as Ministers respond to other demands and expectations and, as pastorates have included more churches, the amount of time Ministers have been able to give to this task has inevitably decreased.

Deep and significant relationships of mutual care and concern enable honesty and transparency and are key to the renewal of the local church, the growth and well-being of individuals and the worshipping community. The local church is not to be renewed as a social centre, or an expression of social life, but a response to spiritual need. Pressure on time and the pace of life limits established ways to health and well-being but spiritual growth requires time and space. This is a serious concern and requires careful attention in discerning priorities and time management. There are no simple answers as Ministry is spread increasingly thinly but the commitment of time to pastoral care in its widest sense of developing health and wholeness in relationships, alongside prayer and study, is essential for the fulfilment of the vocation to Ministry of the Word and Sacraments.

---

44 Willimon, W. H. (ed.) 2002.

The Minister of the Word and Sacraments carries the responsibility for equipping, enabling, developing and nurturing spiritual life, both his or her own and that of those who follow his or her leadership. We might therefore seek to increase the provision of ordained Ministry of the Word and Sacraments, the number of Ministers available to the churches, while maintaining local leadership from within, which is trained and equipped, supported and authorised by the wider Church in order to ensure theological and ecclesiastical integrity and to encourage movement and change but also enables an appropriate contextual response. Every church member, as a disciple and follower of Jesus Christ, must be given opportunities for spiritual growth and development to their own maturity in Christ, and so to respond ever more fully to the call to discipleship and engagement in mission and ministry.

P. T. Forsyth described Ministry as *sacramental* but not *sacerdotal, not merely illuminative but augmentive, not to enlighten simply but to empower and enhance.*[45] This marks a departure from an orthodox Reformed stance, which might recognise the office as sacramental but maintain there are only two Sacraments.

Paul Fiddes, also writing from the Reformed tradition, refers to Austin Farrer's description of the Christian Minister as *walking sacrament,* recognising the blurring of the line between person and function, being and doing but saying, *the vocation to Christian Ministry is a call to a way of being, not just to the exercise of skills or the carrying out of a set of*

---

45 Willimon, W. H. (ed.) 2002 p.134.

functions. Fiddes continues, *they point beyond themselves to some value... and they are expected to embody these values in their lives. Christian pastors are therefore Sacraments of the transcendent grace of love and forgiveness, and the kind of persons they are will be bound up with the things they do. They are 'living symbols' of the sacrificial and persuasive love of Christ.*[46]

Fiddes also refers to Campbell's discussion of the limits of pastoral care and a proper anxiety about unreachable ideals. *In reaction,* he writes, *a pastor may develop a totally functional view of ministry, as if all that matters is the task performed. Yet disaster looms if the link between being and doing is neglected. If a pastor is with people for God at the critical points of sorrow and joy in life, her personality is bound to be shaped by this and in turn to shape the quality of her presence there. And people in fact want someone as their pastor who is open to the mystery of God in the midst of these events and is able to be that for them.*[47]

The Minister of the Word and Sacraments does not claim to be the ideal Christian. Fiddes says, *The whole point of a sacrament is that it is a piece of weak, created, and fallible stuff in itself, but is a doorway into the life of the triune God. Precisely in its frailty the sacrament symbolises an ultimate value. It can embody an ideal without being an ideal.* In concluding his discussion, he refers to the cost of such Ministry in human terms. It is a cost *carried by those willing to be living Sacraments. The sacramental life is one that is open*

---

46 Fiddes, P. 2000 p.294 quoting from *A Celebration of Faith* 1970 p.110.
47 See, for example, Campbell, A. V. 1981.

to the presence of God, and can open a door for others into eternal movements of love and justice that are there ahead of us, and before us, and embracing us. This openness can be felt like the invitation to dance, but sometimes like the raw edges of a wound. This is participation in God. This is theology.[48]

Forsyth suggested *The Church will be what its Ministry makes it*, insisting on the need to deepen understanding of discipleship and vocation rather than for more Ministers, to prevent the Church from becoming *God's frozen people* or a drift to clericalism.[49] Peel expresses the need: *A highly gifted and thoroughly prepared professional Ministry, distinct but never separated from lay people, arguably is the best means there is for creating and empowering the vocation of the whole Church.*[50] Instead, he suggests, too many Ministers are unable to collaborate, and lack teaching ability and theological acumen. He describes the continuing challenge as *to enable and support people to engage in God's mission* which recognises the vocation of every Church member.

He suggests the drive towards more ordained Ministry is putting the cart before the horse and addresses other issues, suggesting that eldership should be freed from the responsibilities of management, a presiding elder be appointed for each church while Ministers are called to Districts[51] rather than churches, and that Non-stipendiary

---

48 Fiddes, P. 2000 p.302.

49 Peel, D. 2007 p.289.

50 Peel, D. 2007 p.290.

51 In the changes that resulted from the review processes involved in "Catch the Vision of God's Tomorrow", the Districts ceased to exist to nearly all intents and purposes (although for legal reasons a District Council continues to be appointed to meet if needed).

Ministry might be seen to be Ministry on the cheap, describing it as *a radical concept largely domesticated.*

There has been some discussion on whether Ministry of the Word and Sacraments belongs to the *"esse"* or the *"bene esse"* of the life of the Church, whether it is essential and constitutive of the life of the Church or necessary for its well-being. In the Reformed understanding, Ministers of the Word and Sacraments are set apart, and any change through ordination is understood as in relationship rather than ontological. Through their ordination Ministers share in a new relationship with the church and the role has both public and representative aspects. Gifts are recognised and developed for the building up of the church but the vocation is neither to functions nor office. Ministers are ordained to relationship, not to task, and ordination confers not power but authorisation for the responsibilities of leadership.

The "normal" Sunday activity in the normal place at the normal time constitutes Church for most Christians. Worship is the core activity of the church's life and preaching and celebration of the Sacraments remain the primary tasks of the Minister, despite significant cultural change from the twentieth into the twenty-first century, for example in Sunday trading and the opening of shops and businesses and places of entertainment, as well as in communication, transport and mobility.

Eugene Petersen writes, *We* (pastors) *are committed to keeping the proclamation* (of God's kingdom here in Jesus) *alive and to looking after souls in a soul-denying soul-*

trivializing age.[52] Forsyth wrote, *men* [sic] *as they leave should be not only clearer but greater, not only surer but stronger, not only interested nor only instructed, nor only affected but fed and increased.*[53] Something is "done" and from that basis it is *Church and preacher that reach the world.* (The preacher) *has to declare the Church's word and to utter the Church's faith, to itself, in order that he* [sic] *and the Church together may declare them to the world.* It is in this way that the local church might be renewed, equipped through the Word and Sacraments for discipleship and witness. Forsyth acknowledged that in preaching the orator brings inspiration and the prophet brings revelation. It is proclamation that is the first charge on the Church.

Peel writes, *Ministers do not seem to devote as much time as they once did to preaching, perhaps putting more faith in other ministerial functions: pastoral care, community work, social activism, or church management.*[54] A Biblical Hebrew textbook supports this view: *From seminaries to denominational headquarters, the prevalent mood and theme is managerial, organizational and psychological* and *curriculum, conferences, seminars and personal example show mastery of the word is not foremost.*[55]

Peel argues for diversity in worship style with cross-fertilisation of traditions and experience and no fixed liturgy from the outset and suggests this was the genius of Cranmer. Worship needs, he suggests, are best served by variety and

---

52 Willimon, W. H. (ed.) 2002 p.91.
53 Willimon, W. H. (ed.) 2002 p.135.
54 Peel, D. 2007 p.211.
55 Pratico, G. D. and Van Pelt, M. V. 2014.

not by prescribed liturgies. There is a need for freedom within order and form. Mind, heart and will are brought to bear to avoid intellectualism, activism or emotionalism and preaching is central which is kerygmatic, expounds scripture, plain in style, sincere, courageous and prophetic, and rooted in pastoral experience. There are demands and standards but delivered with warmth, spontaneity and intimacy with no system imposed from beyond. On this basis worship can be participative, intelligible, and accessible.[56]

Susan Durber, writing from experience of Ministry and theological education, acknowledges that there are questions to be asked about new ways of being a Minister but says, *I have found nothing among some of the recent attempts to redefine Ministry which can compare with the life I promised to lead and the roles I promised to fulfil with God's help at my ordination and at inductions since.*[57] She continues, *At its heart, Ministry is about proclaiming the gospel, breaking bread and sharing wine at the communion table, praying and leading worship, and offering pastoral care and leadership to the church.* She suggests ordination does not result in a change of status but is not only about function, and would also want to resist professionalization. She recognises the significance of call and place: *God finds a way to bring me again to the holy places where people gather, where the Bible is open and where bread and wine are shared. For that is where I can most truly answer the call.*[58]

---

56 Peel, D. 2007.

57 Wootton, J. (ed.) 2007 p.140.

58 Wootton, J. (ed.) 2007 p.141.

CONCLUSION

Beginnings and endings matter. The Church as an institution begins with the Church as it is, but the need for imagination, creativity and change must be acknowledged. Alternatively, we might begin with aspiration, the Church as it might be, and recognise the potential for change from the bottom up rather than top down, from the edge rather than from the centre.[59] The necessary energy and impetus, creativity and imagination for change might indeed come from the edge rather than the centre, but the language itself might have little meaning in a conciliar Church. The core of Church life is always the congregational expression of Christian discipleship, the church where the people are, the local expression of the sign, instrument and foretaste of the kingdom of God. This core is to be resourced and equipped by the Ministry of the Word and Sacraments called, trained, equipped and sent through the wider Church.

The relationships between what might be seen as the "centre" (i.e. Church House and its staff, the Committees of General Assembly and their officers and General Assembly itself, Synods and their officers and Committees), and the "edge" (i.e. local churches and congregations) require urgent attention, decision and action. Local churches experience increasing isolation from wider Church structures and decision-making.

Ministers of the Word and Sacraments embody those relationships and have an important role in their health and

---

59 The qualitative research conducted by George Lings into fresh expressions of Church was published from 1999 in a quarterly booklet, *Encounters on the Edge*.

development. If we are serious about addressing the need for paradigm shift and culture change, we need to discern what in the local church needs to be retained and what must be let go. Time and commitment are required for strategic planning for the longer term, and we may be running out of years. There are no quick fixes, no instant ways of building the Kingdom, of delivering church renewal or growth. Rather, slowly, patiently, prayerfully, carefully, we build relationships that result in faithfulness and fruitfulness as God continues to call individuals and communities.

At this time, the Church, at least in the West, declines numerically; culture change makes its impact and people seek spirituality but not in the Church. T. S. Eliot (1888–1965), writing in very different times in "Choruses from the Rock" has words for this time:

"What life have you if you have not life together?
There is no life that is not in community,
And no community not lived in praise of GOD.
Even the anchorite who meditates alone,
For whom the days and nights repeat the praise of GOD,
Prays for the Church, the Body of Christ incarnate.
And now you live dispersed on ribbon roads,
And no man knows or cares who is his neighbour
Unless his neighbour makes too much disturbance,
But all dash to and fro in motor cars,
Familiar with the roads and settled nowhere.
Nor does the family even move about together,
But every son would have his motor cycle,
And daughters ride away on casual pillions.

Much to cast down, much to build, much to restore;
Let the work not delay, time and the arm not waste;
Let the clay be dug from the pit, let the saw cut the stone,
Let the fire not be quenched in the forge."[60]

Ministry of the Word and Sacraments has been a calling requiring lengthy training but also a commitment to lifelong learning. A solution to the perceived shortage of Ministers of the Word and Sacraments might lie in shorter and more accessible courses but a loss of breadth and depth or rigour might be the inevitable consequence. Yet as technology advances and culture changes, there may be shifts that the Church needs to make. Learning takes place in very different ways. Taking variety and diversity seriously, it will be important to review roles and responsibilities that have become fixed and rigid. Established theology and patterns and practice of Ministry might also require re-examination.

Practice has already changed, in the introduction of Non-stipendiary Ministry (NSM), Church Related Community Work (CRCW) Ministry, and most recently NSM Model 4, exercised in a specific and limited local context, and Non-stipendiary CRCW Ministry. In my previous research into small churches, I explored the development at that time (2006) of Local Ministry in the Church of England and the provision of Local Leadership in the Yorkshire and Mersey Synods of the United Reformed Church. Both now represent established practice across the respective denominations while remaining to some degree problematic.

---

60 Eliot, T.S. 2002. Reproduced with permission of the publisher.

Learning by doing and reflective practice have also been developed and are now essential components of training for ordination alongside the academic study of doctrine, Church history, hermeneutics and so on. It is recognised that theology and practice are of equal importance and they belong together. The understanding of Ministry however goes beyond a narrow consideration of theological training and its impact on individuals. The initial call is heard by the individual; it is tested through the local church, and then by the wider Church. It is developed through recognised training and then confirmed in the invitation of the local church to serve in a particular context with particular people at a particular time, and finally by ordination and induction as a Minister of the United Reformed Church.

The theology and practice of Ministry, the perception of who Ministers are and what they do, impacts the whole Church, through the entire process but does not end there. Learning continues in diverse ways and forms and in the twenty-first-century Church, relationships are key. Ministers work and serve in diverse relationships across local churches and communities. They are not put on a pedestal for the local church to serve, but to equip, empower, challenge, inspire and encourage others to be the church, the sign, instrument and foretaste of the kingdom of God. They point the way, and lead the way, but are not the way.

The leadership they offer should be collaborative and shared with others. This sharing is primarily with elders, who are called locally, and ordained and equipped to share the responsibilities of leadership, to share the gospel, and to build up the body of Christ. The relationships in which and through which Ministers share themselves are also much broader, with church members, with others touched by but on the edge of the church's life, with the wider communities in which the churches they serve are set, and with colleagues and officers in the wider Church, denominationally and ecumenically.

Together Ministers of the Word and Sacraments address the challenges facing today's Church and opportunities to herald the coming of the kingdom. The development of pioneer Ministries and the formation of new ecclesial communities across and beyond denominations begin to demonstrate a future of diverse local leadership. In established congregations, local leadership is being developed, resourced and trained. This might stimulate renewed and focused attention on the significant contribution and often unrealised potential of eldership in the life of the United Reformed Church and its understanding of Ministry. It might also provide a stimulus to ensure that Ministers of the Word and Sacraments are valued, affirmed and supported as well as being equipped and resourced. They will need to discover allies, work collaboratively, and learn from others in church and in community. We may not know what the future church will look like, but we would expect these characteristics: the church, as its Ministry, will continue to be sustained by the scriptures, and strengthened through worship, in dependence on God and in mutual love and care.

QUESTIONS FOR DISCUSSION

- Is the renewal of the local church a priority? What might it look like in a post-pandemic world given current concerns?
- What does it mean to be a "learning Church"? Will it always be an aspiration rather than reality?
- Is there a right balance between the roles of the Minister in relation to the Word and Sacraments, worship, pastoral care, mission and leadership? Which gifts, aptitudes, skills and experience are essential?
- What are the signs of the times for Church and culture and how do the two relate to one another? What are the likely changes in the next generation? What might surprise us?
- How might a focus on building healthy relationships change the expectations of the church and of Ministers?

FOUR

REFLECTION 3

REPORTS TO ASSEMBLY 1982-2017

INTRODUCTION

In *The Story of the Moderators*, David Peel writes: *the Moderators have found themselves managing a pattern of Ministerial deployment known to accelerate rather than arrest congregational decline. In 1981 they concluded that, 'it seems to us that the rationalization of pastorates made necessary by the decrease in the number of Ministers available has gone as far as it can without seriously damaging the leadership that Ministers can give'. But their words went unheeded; the practice continued. No one has invented a better way of encouraging the demise of churches than spreading the Ministerial butter ever more thinly over the ecclesiastical bread. A more focused deployment strategy was desperately needed but it was not forthcoming.*[61]

---

61 Peel, D. 2012 p.56.

If there was a simple, painless and risk-free solution to the discernment of vocations and deployment of the Ministry of the Word and Sacraments in the United Reformed Church, it would have been found by now. Yet the reports to its General Assembly proposing change which I consider here (particularly "Patterns of Ministry", "Equipping the Saints" and "Challenge to the Church") have met with a similar response. It is recognised that if we keep on doing the same things, we get the same results, but no way has yet been found to break the cycle. Rather than embrace the risks and carry the consequences of strategic and systematic development and change, decisions are made and practices adopted piecemeal and ad hoc, in a reactive rather than proactive manner. The denomination, the Church as institution, has repeatedly sought, through reports and resolutions arising from them, to break the cycle which leads to the demise of churches, but decisions in the Councils of the Church have not opened paths to renewal for the local church.

Change must come from or at least be owned by the churches. If experiment is the way forward, local churches carry the risks. There are also significant governance issues to be addressed for change to take place in an institution with the decision-making processes and conciliar government of the United Reformed Church. One way forward might be for approaches to be initiated at the local level with support available through Synod and General Assembly. Some Synods do make financial resources available to local churches for innovation, but financial support is not the only form of support that is needed.

I have considered "What are Ministers for?". The expectations of the churches, and probably among Ministers themselves, and of the Church as an institution, are clear. Ministers lead worship, preside at the Sacraments, provide pastoral care, and give leadership to the church for its mission and service in the world. This may offer an unchanged and unchanging shape of Ministry, but the context of this Ministry, in both the world and the Church, is very different compared with a generation ago, and the challenges the church faces are different too. The pattern of Ministry in which every church is provided with ordained Ministry and one Minister serves one church is no longer sustainable, but there is little evidence that the grouping of churches with a single Minister has resulted in effective collaboration or partnership. The same mindset prevails, the same thinking dominates – and it is perhaps telling that pioneer Ministry often works with the same model.

PREPARING TODAY FOR TOMORROW'S MINISTRY (1982)[62]

The report "Preparing today for tomorrow's Ministry" was brought to General Assembly in 1982. It followed discussion in the 1973 Assembly which resulted in the Commission on the Ministry in 1975 and a review in 1980. The large review group, representing a wide range of views and experience, was chaired by Lesslie Newbigin and included Ministers, Moderators, ordinands and others.[63] They declared, "now is the time to press for action".

---

62 United Reformed Church 1982.
63 Richard Church (an ordinand at the time), Michael Davis, Peter Jupp, Janet Sowerbutts, and Bernard Thorogood were among the members of the group.

The report described the Church as the sign, instrument and forecast of God's reign, called into a holy priesthood. It described the established pattern of leadership of leaders who create followers who themselves become leaders. There is a movement from priests to the priesthood of all and from Ministers to all sharing in ministry. All are followers in corporate witness engaging in mission in the community. All are called. This is reflected in the Basis of Union with particular reference to baptism and the link between promises made then and on becoming a Church member.

The report emphasised the urgency of the call of God, which is unchanging in a changing world. The task of those ordained to Ministry of the Word and Sacraments is to equip and enable the whole Church. Leadership is based in servanthood but there are different styles of leadership.

The report described the gospel as an expression of God's reign and not about the success of the Church. It suggests these qualifications as fundamental to Ministry:

1. Commitment to Christ and experience of shared life in the Spirit
2. Growing understanding of the Bible and tradition
3. Involvement in issues of the contemporary world
4. Not one style of Ministry – varied gifts, temperaments and abilities
5. Collaboration and teamwork
6. Communication
7. Through life learning

It focused on the content of college-based training, suggesting Ministry is for a range of contexts and recommending training as required in three areas:

A. DISCIPLESHIP

Attention is necessary to spiritual development, to a "prayer-shaped hole in the heart" as well as a "study-shaped hole in the head". Ministry requires devotion and theology; Bible study, prayer and spiritual direction all have a part to play. Discipleship is the background for leading worship and interpersonal relations, for a "fully human life".

B.UNDERSTANDING

Ministry engages personal experience of God and commitment to God's will in the world and the challenges from other Christians, other faiths and contemporary human situations. Doing theology is shaped by culture and Ministerial formation is a dialectical process involving text and context. Training should therefore involve placements in secular and Church contexts as well as study of the Bible, Church history, systematic theology, other faiths and ideologies such as modernism and Marxism, and ethics.

C. SKILLS

Ministers need to know and do more about more. There is a range of appropriate skills – handling the Bible, public speaking, relating to age groups, dealing with mental illness or stress, working with difference, dealing with statutory and voluntary agencies and the media, non-verbal communication as well as leading public worship and evangelism. Working collaboratively, handling responsibility and expectations, leading appropriately, and managing people and situations also require self-criticism and self-awareness.

It is clear that forms but not necessarily content of training have changed over time. Greater importance is now attached to the practice of lifelong learning, through Education for Ministry phases 2 and 3 (EM2 and EM3). I suggest greater continuity and consistency now from EM1 (which might be residential or non-residential but continues to be delivered through colleges),[64] to EM2 and EM3 is of crucial importance and would benefit Ministers and churches.

The report divided the course of training into three parts, a "foundation" period, and periods pre- and post-foundation.

In the pre-foundation period, the emphasis is on the individual. In the "foundation" period there are four emphases – collaborative skills, group leadership, ecumenical sharing and the context of secular struggles for justice and freedom. An extended programme of placements in secular settings was proposed. The report also recommended the pooling of resources between colleges, so that resources could be used economically and students might work together. (Nearly

---

64 Following the recommendations of the 2006 Training Review, the colleges were reduced to three in number (in Scotland, Cambridge and Manchester) and came to be referred to as Resource Centres for Learning (or RCLs).

forty years on, there is discussion of integration in theological education in the United Reformed Church, but now with significantly reduced resources particularly of people and finance.) Familiarity with the denomination's Departments, Councils and Committees would also be developed in this formation period and there would be opportunities for overseas study and exchange.

In the third, "post-formation", phase the commitment to lifelong learning would be reinforced with guidance and challenge. Ministers would be appointed to an assistantship, with a colleague in a single pastorate, to a team, or to a Local Ecumenical Partnership. There would be supervision and a system of regular reporting.

On the satisfactory completion of two years in the post-formation phase and after a refresher event, the Minister would move into "In Service Training". Seven days' concentrated study was recommended, with financial provision, and sabbatical study was also encouraged with colleges in Cambridge, Manchester and Oxford, Wales and Birmingham as resources. The pattern of training locations current at the time would continue with the opportunity for experiment with decentralised, non-residential training while the colleges would be resource and teaching centres for the whole Church.

The report also referred to recruitment, assessment and selection but there was no reference to deployment. The proposals would cost £70,000, which would be raised through the Unified Appeal, the scheme of the time through which giving from local Churches provided the finances for ordained Ministry in the churches.

This was the world into which I was ordained and began Ministry in the United Reformed Church, training alongside Methodists and Anglicans at the Queen's College in Birmingham between 1983 and 1986. There has been some response to the report's proposals over the years but with the benefit of hindsight the report reads strangely now. In 1982, there was perhaps writing on the wall and we were running out of years. Congregations had been declining for a considerable period of time and churches had closed. Churches were being grouped to be served by a single Minister and Local Ecumenical Partnerships were being established in increasing numbers.

Today, the core curriculum for training and the role of the Minister of the Word and Sacraments are very similar. There is considerable common ground between the seven qualifications above and the expectations (or Marks) of Ministry agreed by Assembly Mission Council in May 2019 (see also Reflection 2). This is in spite of substantial change in Church and culture and significant changes and new patterns of Ministry, including the introduction of Non-stipendiary Ministry (NSM) and team Ministry, group pastorates, Church Related Community Work (CRCW) Ministry and Elders in Local Leadership. The appointment of Training and Development Officers (TDOs) and similar posts in the Synods has also been a consequence of greater emphasis on and attention to ongoing training and lifelong learning for Ministers and for the whole Church, but has perhaps deflected resources, energy and attention away from the Minister's role as theological educator and trainer in and for the congregation.

PATTERNS OF MINISTRY (1995)[65]

According to the "Patterns of Ministry" Report, between 1973 and the 1990s the membership decline in the United Reformed Church was forty-two per cent, while the number of churches had decreased by thirteen per cent and the number of Ministers by thirty-four per cent. In 1974 the ratio of churches to Ministers was 1.8:1 but by 1993 it had risen to 2.3:1. The appointment of Non-stipendiary Ministers had gone some way to fill the gaps but there was variation in their availability and geographical distribution. In any case, it was clear the single pastorate was no longer normative and spreading Ministers more thinly was not a satisfactory response.

The report recognised that Ministers were "servants of the Word so that the saints of God might be built up in the ministry given to all God's people through the many gifts of the Spirit for the work of Christ"[66] and that Ministry should be shared, collaborative and related to context. District Councils, it said, "will wish to deploy Ministers in the most creative way".[67] The way was open to flexibility but a pattern was emerging of joint pastorates with evidence of a lack of leadership in local churches placing increased and potentially impossible burdens on Ministers. The report included proposals to introduce collaborative Ministry imaginatively and flexibly, responding to needs and opportunities in local churches and communities. Tucker describes the report as *a significant theological milestone*[68]

---

65 United Reformed Church 1995.

66 United Reformed Church 1995 p.115.

67 United Reformed Church 1995 p.117.

68 Tucker, T. 2003.

but looking back I suggest it might be more accurately perceived as a lost opportunity.

District Councils were themselves subsequently abolished in the changes resulting from the "Catch the Vision of God's Tomorrow"[69] review presented to General Assembly in 2006. With hindsight, this change itself limited flexibility and increased the isolation of local churches and the feeling of distance from the Synod. It was at the Synod level where it was perceived decisions were being made and where resources and expertise might be accessed. In response to the statistics, it might also be argued that the closure of churches was an inevitable consequence of numerical decline and the continuing trend. I point out resistance in local churches is also inevitable to proposals to close from outside the local church.

The issues of establishing criteria of viability, mission potential, and kingdom value need to be carefully addressed. Further, the unity of a conciliar Church might be severely tested if decisions made in the Councils do not draw on local support. In any case it is paramount that the Councils of the Church exist to serve the local churches, and not vice versa.

There is some evidence of pressure for Ministry to be allocated to an area rather than a local church or pastorate. Such a change in practice would have serious implications for the Reformed understanding of call and invitation. Councils might also use or be given (there is some debate about the content of the Basis of Union) their authority to close

---

69 https://urc.org.uk/images/bltg/catch-the-vision-from-assembly_report_06.pdf [accessed 24th May 2021].

churches, to "deploy" Ministers or to take other decisions that have a profound and lasting effect on the life and witness of local churches. I would argue that the knowledge and experience of the local context is of crucial importance in decision-making and must always be taken seriously.

The report suggested the wider context of social change required varied Ministries, with missionary calling the overriding consideration. The Working Party Report (1995) suggested that Ministry is focused in the world for the world for God's sake. The first task was therefore to discern the will of God for mission in each place and to provide Ministry appropriate to the needs and opportunities.

The report recognised a need for a spectrum of Ministries with different functions and styles, working collaboratively without a hierarchy, within which Non-stipendiary Ministry might be understood as Local Ministry, authorised to serve in a designated pastorate or congregation. Ministry through work in the world was also a possibility, although an uncertain relationship with the Councils of the Church might be a consequence. Currently, NSM4 and Non-stipendiary Church Related Community Work Ministry offer these dimensions of Ministry in new ways, but, I would argue, they do not present a strategic approach to the issues and challenges the Church faces but are being developed and deployed piecemeal and ad hoc.

Lay preaching and Church Related Community Work Ministry were affirmed. A change to the term "Local Preacher" was also proposed but not accepted. Two principles were affirmed in relation to presidency at the Sacraments: the Sacraments linked the local church to the whole Church and local congregations should be sensitive to the ecumenical dimension. This represents a continuing and persistent issue that has arisen frequently in the churches without reaching a resolution that satisfies all – how are the Sacraments, as God's gift to the Church, made available to the local church when the number of Ministers of the Word and Sacraments is declining?

In the light of the experience of the Churches of Christ, it had been proposed previously that presiding elders might provide local leadership in each place. This proposal had been rejected on the grounds that it would create a new tier of Ministry and result in division. "Patterns of Ministry" proposed an alternative: one or more "moderating elders" would provide stimulus, leadership and initiative. They would be local representatives with a diminished sacramental role, and focus on pastoral care. Some might lead worship and chair meetings.

General Assembly rejected the proposal for moderating elders. The United Reformed Church was clearly not ready for a local Ministry working collaboratively. It was perceived that the proposals devalued ordained Ministry, and no training was in place for collaborative styles. The consequences are however now clear, with Ministers of the Word and Sacraments serving larger groupings of churches and elders bearing increasing responsibility. Tucker suggests the proposals were too optimistic and the model of Ministry practised by the Churches of Christ, around half of whose congregations in the United Kingdom had joined the United Reformed Church in 1981, had not been adequately assimilated. At the same time, there was uncertainty about the expansion of Non-stipendiary Ministry.

Tucker states the report's *challenges could not be ignored and the issues which it had highlighted of the development and deployment of Ministerial resources would continue to occupy the Councils of the Church*.[70] They have done and continue to do so, and not only the Councils but the churches too as pastorates have been continually reshaped and reorganized and the pattern of spreading Ministers more and more thinly has continued in spite of the evidence that this is detrimental to Ministers and to the churches they serve.

EQUIPPING THE SAINTS (2004)[71]

The "Patterns of Ministry" report sought to respond to the challenge to the United Reformed Church to provide leadership and Ministry of the Word and Sacraments to the local church in the face of declining membership, the diminishing number of Ministers and the reducing level of financial resources. In 1997 a statement on the theology of ministry was accepted by Mission Council. In 1998 guidelines for Local Church Leaders were agreed, with encouragement to experiment, and in 1999 the "Growing Up" mission strategy, with a focus on church growth, was adopted. In 2001, groups and joint pastorates had been defined with reference to clusters and local mission partnerships with a variety of possibilities for the relationship between the Minister and congregation.

---

70 Tucker, T. 2003 p.184.

71 United Reformed Church 2004 (Reports to General Assembly from 2003 onwards are also available at https://urc.org.uk/general-assembly/1158-general-assembly-archive.html) [accessed 24th April 2020].

A working group on Ministerial deployment described the perception of a shortage of Ministers as "inaccurate and unhelpful". This perception focused perhaps on a past model of church life which could not be replicated in the present and might also lead to a loss of vision and confidence in local churches and would not encourage local churches to look to their own resources.

Today, ongoing and currently very focused discussions and proposals relating to deployment make local leadership and the role of elders even more significant. I suggest that there are alternative approaches. We cannot begin with a blank sheet of paper, but a substantial review might provide a basis for more joined-up decision-making across the whole Church. Such a review would necessarily include an open, honest and accurate audit of the resources available, of people, finance, plant, gifts, aptitudes and experience and a prayerful exploration of opportunities and potential. A strategic model of the deployment of Ministry might then be developed in the light of opportunities and needs discerned under the guidance of the Holy Spirit through prayer and reflection.[72]

Rather than assessing viability and sustainability too narrowly with preconceptions and prejudices, it would be possible to provide for a variety of responses depending on

---

72 Written and prepared for publication before Mission Council resolutions agreed to set up the Church Life Review. See United Reformed Church, 2021. *Future of the Church*. [Online] Available at https://urc.org.uk/images/MissionCouncil/March-2021/A1_Future_of_the_URC.pdf [accessed 15th July 2022] and United Reformed Church, 2021. *Church Life Review*. [Online] Available at https://urc.org.uk/wp-content/uploads/1638/27/Paper_N2_-_Church_Life_Review.pdf [accessed 15th July 2022].

context. An Appreciative Inquiry approach, which focuses on the positive rather than deficit models, might be adopted. Instead of the analysis of strengths, weaknesses, opportunities and threats (SWOT) which tends to focus on the negative, Appreciative Inquiry opens up potential through the analysis of strengths, opportunities, aspirations and resources (SOAR).[73]

Response to decline had been to place Ministers of the Word and Sacraments in pastoral charge of groups of small congregations in dispersed communities. This practice raised issues in relation to the leadership of churches in their engagement in God's mission and the impact on the Ministers themselves. There were other factors to consider. The pool of potential candidates was declining against the increasing rate of Ministers retiring. There was a reducing number of lay preachers and their age profile was increasing. Eighty-five per cent of the denomination's budget was being spent on Ministers' stipends and training and costs of Ministry continued to grow. With regard to presidency at the Sacraments, there was diversity of practice which was not always in line with policy.

If the renewal of the local church is to come through the Word and Sacraments, change is necessary and urgent. In 2002 the "Catch the Vision for God's Tomorrow" review[74] had introduced considerable structural change. Discussion arising from the circulation of the interim "Equipping the Saints" report focused on the ministry of the whole people of God, which was interpreted in diverse ways while maintaining the importance of ordained Ministry and leadership.

---

73 https://appreciating.Church/ [accessed 24th May 2021].

74 https://urc.org.uk/images/bltg/catch-the-vision-from-assembly_report_06.pdf [accessed 24th May 2021].

The final "Equipping the Saints" report was wide-reaching and made a number of recommendations which were generally accepted. It sought to provide support for the church when gathered for fellowship and worship and dispersed in discipleship, witness and mission. In particular it explored more effective use of Ministers of the Word and Sacraments. It stated, "We are convinced that the practice of spreading Ministers ever more thinly, without fundamentally changing the expectations of what the Ministers can and should do, is not the best mission strategy."[75] It suggested that expectations needed to be challenged and changed and recognised that the earlier undertaking to provide Ministry to every Church was unsustainable. Effective leadership was needed in every place, so imagination and collaboration were necessary, with flexibility in training, funding and deployment. Re-thinking was again recommended with regard to presidency at the Sacraments.

Note was taken of the social context; there was a growing lack of involvement in religion in people's busy lives, and diverse demands on their time and energy. God's mission was unchanging but the context of that mission was changing with the world in an almost continuous state of flux.

"Patterns of Ministry" had focused on more effective missionary engagement as a basis for Ministerial deployment. General Assembly at that time had continued to support a single order of Ministry, and rejected the proposals for Moderating Elders, Local Ministers and Local Preachers. New proposals now made wide reference to the life of the United Reformed Church, and to diverse forms of ministry and

---

75 United Reformed Church 2004 p.129.

leadership. The expressed aim was to "refocus the Church on its participation in God's mission to the world and to equip all the members of the Church, the whole people of God, to play a fuller part in the continuing ministry of the Lord Jesus Christ".

The report made a commitment to the development of elders,[76] including taking the Basis of Union more seriously. Eldership is central to the life of the United Reformed Church. Its function and operation are locally focused and collaborative. Elders, supported by the Minister of the Word and Sacraments, have primary responsibility for oversight and leadership, sharing the vision of the community of God's people in a particular place. The Minister is a member of the elders' meeting, and with the elders offers representative ministry in the local community.

I point out that in a group pastorate the Minister cannot belong to or share the identity of every local community. The Minister might focus on equipping the elders for their roles and responsibilities of pastoral oversight and leadership. I also suggest attention needs to be given to the process of appointment of elders – election, preparation, ordination – and their continuing learning and development. Other forms of service might also be offered, supported and facilitated by Synods and Areas, while authority continues to lie with the church meeting in each place.

2004 General Assembly agreed four resolutions, welcoming the "Equipping the Saints" report, and challenging every congregation to respond locally to its first two recommendations; firstly to "review its life at all levels with the specific aim of being more supportive and enabling the

---

76 Discussion of the 2007 Eldership report follows.

dispersed ministry of its members even if this means doing less 'in-church' activities" and secondly "to explore new ways of gathering at different times and places". Comments on the recommendations on other matters, including eldership and Local Church Leadership were invited from churches, Area and District Councils and Synods. It was agreed that further work should be undertaken by the Ministries Committee, in co-operation with the Catch the Vision Review Group, to bring formal proposals to General Assembly in 2005.

2005 General Assembly received a summary of the 2004 report and the 2004 recommendations. It was suggested that neither a standard pattern nor a hierarchy of patterns would enable the best possible support or the use of particular gifts. An "honest and explicit discussion between Ministers and others to identify agreed, realistic expectations concerning the particular Minister's unique calling" was needed, with regular review. Ministry might be devalued as "maintenance" but a wide variety of patterns could exist. It was agreed that the identification of those patterns was the responsibility of the Councils and not the Assembly Committee. Resolutions on eldership, collaborative leadership, deployment and financial reporting were carried and "Catch the Vision" would continue to undertake its wider review.

I suggest that "Equipping the Saints" brought very little fundamental change and had little or no impact on or consequences for the churches or their Ministers. Some changes were introduced following the report's recommendations, for example in the detail of record keeping and classification of Ministers. Other change would await developments elsewhere, particularly the implications of the Church of England Hind process, which sought to promote a learning Church, but also ultimately achieved very little. In some areas of church life, lay preaching for example, there was no change. The issue of remuneration was not pursued.

There is an apparent reluctance to move forward, perhaps because there is no ownership of such reports by the local churches whose needs they seek to serve. Resolutions have repeatedly been rejected by the General Assembly or, when passed, not been taken forward into the life of the churches, even if there have been considerable time and energy expended on processes of consultation to promote ownership. Whether the responsibility is ascribed to "Church House", the "General Secretariat", or to Councils and Committees this is a substantial cause for concern.

The situation may be an indication of the attitudes of the kind of people appointed as representatives or the Ministers themselves. The Councils of the Church may be conservative and resistant to change or there may be little appetite or incentive for change across the churches. Alternatively, local churches may have different priorities and perspectives, or a different vision from the ideas developed in denominational Committees, task groups or Church House. There is also some evidence of doubt, even suspicion, in local churches that denominational officers do not always have their best interests at heart, although those officers claim, rightly, that they are also members of local churches. An underlying factor may be simple indifference. The local church does not recognise the significance or relevance of the activity of the wider Church.[77]

---

77 Thanks to Robert Pope for this point.

In the face of severe and consistent threat and the harsh realities of decline, maintaining the status quo in local churches makes fewer demands. Resistance to change may be rooted in inertia or a need to find security in the known rather than risk the unknown. Mark Oakley suggests that for individuals the ego seeks to form identity from past and present and is fearful for the future. The God of transformation however is to be found outside the wall.[78] This relates to individual change but might also be applied to communities.

It might be argued that denominational initiatives and resources (for example, Mission Pursuit in the 1980s, and, more recently, Vision4Life and Vision 2020) have had little lasting impact for the majority of individuals and churches. This is not to offer a counsel of despair but to recognise the extent of the challenge. More recently, the "Walking the Way" initiative has focused on individual discipleship but also sought to implement a change of mindset across the denomination. It is difficult at this stage to assess its impact on church life.[79]

Attention must be given to issues of communication from the centre to the edge and from the edge to the centre. Ways need to be found for voices to be heard, and channels of communication established for open and honest speaking and listening. The issues of the management of change in a conciliar Church need to be addressed and it is vital to hear as many voices as possible.

---

78 Oakley, M. 2019 p.6.
79 https://urc.org.uk/our-work/walking-the-way.html [accessed 24th May 2021].

TRAINING REVIEW (2006)[80]

In 2006, the Training Department (in the terms and structure of the time) of the United Reformed Church undertook a thorough review of provision and practice. Assembly accepted its proposals; training for ordained Ministry in the United Reformed Church, which had been provided at a number of centres non-residentially as well as residentially, would be limited to Northern College in Manchester, Westminster College in Cambridge and the Scottish College. Principles agreed in 2005 that training should be "integrated, ecumenical and Reformed" were endorsed and new steps were proposed and agreed. Resources would be concentrated, partnerships would be developed with wholehearted but realistic ecumenical engagement. It was claimed that the proposals were on educational and ecumenical grounds and not driven by financial considerations although the financial background was provided in considerable detail in an appendix. In conclusion it was stated that the proposals would provide "better expression of the importance of learning for the whole Church"[81] against a background of good stewardship.

The review had included extensive consultation processes. Facing continuing and significant decline in membership and in the number of Ministerial candidates there was an opportunity, God-given, for renewal and radical change. The intention was to promote lifelong learning for the whole people of God while integrating

---

80   United Reformed Church 2006 pp.109 ff.
81   United Reformed Church 2006 p.126.

the training of Ministers. Currently, "integration" is a key word in ongoing discussion and review in the Education and Learning Committee of the United Reformed Church. I suggest there was (and continues to be) scope for training institutions and providers to work more closely together, and certainly in collaboration rather than in competition with one another. The co-ordination of training, education and learning across the Resource Centres for Learning (RCLs) and including the Synods has considerable potential to enhance the provision and benefit all stakeholders, individual Ministers, preachers and elders, churches and Synods, as well as the RCLs. Complete integration may not be possible, necessary or beneficial but collaboration and continuity should be developed. Proposals in relation to management and governance should take the significance of local factors and distinctiveness into account.

The review also referred to the Regional Training Partnerships, initiated by the Church of England following its own review, and the Hind Report.[82] The Partnerships were subsequently abandoned and followed by the development of Common Awards in 2014. There were also separate developments in Scotland and Wales, which were outside the remit of the Hind Report.

The review proposed: the three "Colleges" should be termed "Resource Centres for Learning" (RCLs) providing "reformed, theological, biblical, historical and educational expertise" to the training scene; the Training Committee would support

---

82 Formation for Ministry within a Learning Church Ministries Division 2000.

partnerships including the Training for Learning and Serving Courses, Synods and the Windermere Centre; the Northern and Westminster RCLs would develop lay training and dispersed learning and with the Scottish College provide all training in the Education for Ministry 1 (initial training for ordination) phase; attention would be given to other relationships.

These reasons were given: the number of students, the need to develop confidence in the tradition, the fact that the three colleges were already a resource, and the potential to develop expertise.

It is beyond doubt that there had been significant change in the landscape from 1982, changes that I have witnessed and experienced particularly in the impact in the West Midlands Synod where I have served continuously since 1986, but also in the wider Church. It was necessary to grasp the nettle and make changes in the provision of training. There were perhaps unavoidable costs. The decision to withdraw training from Mansfield College in Oxford and from some ecumenical and particularly Church of England non-residential courses across the country was quite readily accepted but opposition was voiced from the West Midlands Synod and the Queen's College in particular, and from the South-west Synod and the South-west Training Course. In both cases, it was argued the changes reduced accessibility to training through the loss of local provision.

The review took account of changes that had taken and were taking place and was prepared to be proactive in making further changes and promoting and supporting change. There is evidence of progress: the Resource Centres for Learning have broadened their provision, particularly in elders' and lay preacher training. Westminster College and Northern College offer lay preaching events and other training opportunities which are advertised independently. I suggest more co-ordination might increase participation and reduce the perception that there is competition between them.

Lifelong learning for the whole Church remains the responsibility of the Education and Learning Committee. The resources and expertise of the RCLs are not as well used as they might be. I suggest an ongoing need for conversation, co-operation and collaboration, for greater continuity and consistency and more joined-up thinking. This should include the Synods and their appointed officers and encompass training for Ministers in EM2 and EM3, elders, lay preachers and potentially the whole Church. Recent discussion of the potential for the integration of training proposes a body to oversee, co-ordinate and undertake curriculum planning with representatives from all the stakeholders.

The review made no reference to previous reports. I presume they had no brief to do so but there was a lost opportunity to include discussion of the theology and practice of Ministry, to revisit proposals that had been previously rejected by General Assembly and to respond to the issues around deployment that the Moderators had recognised as early as 1981. Patterns of Ministry determine training requirements, on the basis of the understanding and practice of Ministry, but also ecclesiology and missiology.

ELDERSHIP (2007)[83]

2007 General Assembly had received a report on eldership after work in Committees had led to a conference. The ministry of elders was valued, working together with Ministers of the Word and Sacraments. Earlier resolutions (from 2005) on calling, training, equipping and development were endorsed but a number of concerns were expressed in relation to the meaning of call and election of elders and their preparation, ongoing training and development, support and accountability. The practice of ordination was maintained, encouraged by the request for clarity, even at the cost of convenience, from ecumenical partners.

It was stated that the grace of God creates the community of disciples, the worshipping community, the sign and instrument of God's kingdom of love and justice in the world. All have a part to play in the common task, with vocation according to gift. Some are called to Ministerial office, and set apart for Ministry of the Word and Sacraments and pastoral oversight, which in the Reformed tradition is shared with elders. Ministers of the Word and Sacraments ensure that the faith is passed on, share responsibility together in the Councils of the Church, and are accountable for the worship and mission of the Church. They provide for the discernment and nurture of gifts, and preside at the Lord's table.

Elders are called and committed to lead the local church with responsibility for worship, fellowship, mission and

---

83   United Reformed Church 2007.

service.[84] Their pattern of ministry is servanthood as seen in Jesus. They work collegially and collaboratively, developing and extending Christian influence in society. They share a diversity of gifts, enabling nurture and discipleship as effective witness. They are called from within, ordained for life but serve for a fixed term.

There are different models evident over time. In 1990 the World Alliance of Reformed Churches (subsequently the World Communion of Reformed Churches) Consultation on Eldership agreed that there was no single order in scripture but scripture gives guidance for practice. The starting point was the message of salvation and the call to mission, leading to discernment of necessary tasks and the choosing of leaders.

The Eldership Report suggested that there are three groups of tasks, each of which needs to be addressed fully, relating to the sacramental life (worship, prayer, obedience), the diaconal function (service) and management. The report also suggested that Ministers are crucial to the nature and purpose of the Church but went on to state: "In a Church where Ministers of the Word and Sacraments are scarce, and vacancies long, we will increasingly need a dedicated and equipped eldership to maintain and enhance the life and mission of the congregation." More recently, General Assembly 2016 agreed the appointment of "authorised elders",[85] with authority to preside at the Sacraments.

The report stated that the burden of pastoral care is changing and there is a growing need to communicate

---

84 See earlier comment and discussion in Reflection 2.
85 United Reformed Church 2016.

to those outside the Church. Elders need to be well prepared and supported for the tasks and responsibilities they undertake. Urgent attention also needs to be given to the identification of new elders and to training and development for all to deepen the understanding of call and ordination to a new relationship, "that setting apart appropriate for ministries which have been established, through testing over time, as central to the life of the Church". Ministers and elders together "will feed the people of God and take responsibility for pastoral care, spiritual health and the discernment and nurture of God-given gifts and talents in others".[86] I suggest that Ministers have a role in discerning the gifts of individuals who might be called to serve as elders, in offering support and encouragement and providing necessary preparation and training. I also suggest the relationship between eldership and Ministers needs more careful examination.

The report indicated that there was further work to be done in several areas: on good practice in the identification, preparation and development of elders; in the conduct, content and oversight of elders' meetings; on the theological distinction between ordination and commissioning; on the biblical roots of language and practice; on the consequences of lay presidency; on continuity and change in ecumenical understandings of ordination; on liturgies and the link with theological intentions and ecclesiology; and on the role of Ministers and elders together in initiation. I have found no record of this work being done.

---

86 United Reformed Church 2007 p.140.

The overarching principles are clear but practicability might be in question. It is recognised that eldership has a vital contribution to make to the life of the local United Reformed Church but this has not always been the case in practice. It is of crucial importance that elders work collaboratively to form an effective team to fulfil the functions of the elders' meeting, but that the elders' meeting does not become either a management or an executive committee. The core purpose of the elders' meeting is to provide spiritual leadership and pastoral care for the local church, leading, equipping and empowering the Church in its calling to share in God's mission under the guidance and in the gift and power of the Holy Spirit.

CHALLENGE TO THE CHURCH (2008)[87]

In 2008 "Challenge to the Church" recognised that more recruitment of Ministers was necessary and certificates of eligibility were agreed. It was acknowledged that the "Equipping the Saints" report and the "Catch the Vision" process had been visionary but conducted against a background of continuing decline. A new challenge was presented to develop new patterns of Ministry. There were four factors associated with growing congregations: quality of worship with a depth of spirituality; a small group culture, nurturing and developing gifts; clarity of purpose; strong local leadership. Pastorates however were continuing to increase in size, limiting the opportunity for Ministers to think and plan, to reflect or to dig deep into the treasures of theology

---

87   United Reformed Church 2008.

and biblical studies. At the same time, congregations were not being encouraged or enabled to grow in their own faith and understanding.

It was suggested Ministry teams might have potential. A strategic approach might support, encourage and develop growing churches, create fresh patterns of Christian presence, recast the less lively, and establish new groups and networks. Such an approach required ministry that equips and enables groups towards mutual support and nurture, corporate witness and service and making a difference as dispersed church. Local leadership would need to be based in a Synod strategy, involving Ministers and elders. Individuals with a pastoral and teaching role would be recognised, providing continuity and a community focus. This might be a Stipendiary or self-supporting (Non-stipendiary) Minister, an elder or lay preacher or a specifically identified Local Church Leader. Team pastorates would be established with flexible leadership patterns, planning worship, nurture and training, with one member providing oversight.

There were issues to be addressed – finding, calling, or recruiting Local Church Leaders to lead worship, provide nurture, and develop witness and service, and Ministers to give pastoral and oversight ministry to groups of congregations, leading from a skill set in theology, biblical studies, training and leadership. Synods would encourage the development of team pastorates and mission opportunities, and establish the criteria for scoping with regular review.

The report recognised the need for further work relating to the Assessment Board, Ministries and Education and Learning Committees; papers would be produced and a three-year timescale was set. Assembly agreed an amended resolution but it does not appear that the radical thinking on strategic approaches to Ministry, looking towards outcomes rather than established practice, was taken forward. I suggest the inherent conservatism of conciliar structures and decision-making is again apparent, holding the status quo and limiting or at least delaying the implementation of change. Consideration needs to be given to how we hold to the values that underpin our theology and practice but allow the necessary flexibility for exploration and the initiation of change in response to challenge.

RESOURCING MINISTRY (2012)[88]

Proposals were brought to the 2012 General Assembly on the resourcing of Ministry. Through Ministry and Mission (M&M) it was stated, "the whole Ministry of the United Reformed Church is to be made available to the whole of the Church". Financial responsibility is shared and deployment of Ministry is not constrained by the availability of local finance. There are particular challenges if we do not recognise that all we have is a gift from God and the model is defined by grace, abundance and mission.

Ministries Committee presented these principles: all are paid the same; there is parity of status; expenses are reimbursed; calling is dependent on support of the Church; the stipend is to enable a reasonable standard of life.

In March 2011 three scenarios for the future of the United Reformed Church had been presented:

---

88   United Reformed Church 2012.

- No change.
- Mixed economy in which Synods are given stipends to be deployed. Posts are open only to Ministers of the Word and Sacraments. Special Category Ministries continue with a maximum number of posts per Synod. Stipends are paid from central funds but other costs are met from Synod, from the pastorate or in other ways. Grants would be available from central funds for further ordained Ministry or for lay ministry.
- The M&M payments are collected but Synods are given a block grant. Special Category Ministries would end but other roles might be developed. Housing and local costs would be a pastorate responsibility, but denominational funds would provide for pensions, in-service training, loans and grants.

A Working Party was set up. Mission Council discussed and broadly welcomed the proposals, the flexibility and diversity they offered and the potential release of creativity, alongside accountability. The likely constraints however were the impact on Ministers and the risks to them, their posts and their livelihoods, the impact on ecumenical relationships, and the limits to Synod responsibility and capacity. In the end, the discussions were not taken forward.

CONCLUSION

We have moved a long way from 1982, and 1995 is over twenty-five years ago. We may have heard what the Spirit is saying to the churches but we need to continue to listen well. The Spirit speaks to individuals and is tested in the Councils of the Church, church meetings, Synod meetings and General Assembly. No clear message relating to change in the shape and practice of Ministry has been heard and the need has been expressed through the churches and Councils for more of the same, more Ministry, while the Ministry that can be provided depends both on financial support and on candidates, and the pool of both is shrinking.

The *wind blows where it chooses* (John 3:8, *NRSV*). There is change, but also resistance to change. New models have been and are being developed in response to the Holy Spirit, equipping and enabling the Church to be the Church, the sign, instrument and foretaste of the kingdom of God, in a world that is changing rapidly sociologically, politically, economically and technologically. Change around us brings challenge and opportunity for change within us and through us. Ministers are still a vital resource – the proclamation of the Word and the celebration of the Sacraments give life to the Church – but new models of leadership might be appropriate for this age, and need to emerge for such a time as this, to work with and alongside them. Ministers and elders will need to work together to bring renewal, health and new life to local churches. A strategic approach to Ministry is needed, which serves the needs of all local churches, responds to diversity of context and opportunity, and offers appropriate challenge. The life of the denomination in its Councils and Committees, its systems and structures must provide flexibility and consistency, while addressing with honesty, integrity and sensitivity the issues, challenges and opportunities of life, death and resurrection in the churches.

QUESTIONS FOR DISCUSSION

- What, generally and specifically, is the impact in the local church of reports and reviews presented to General Assembly?

- How does the local church influence the wider Church? Why is the wider Church often perceived and described as "them" and not "us"?

- What freedom and readiness for change is there in local churches? What are the obstacles? Are there alternative ways to implement change?

- How far does the wider Church reflect the views and concerns of local churches? Is communication important? How might it be improved?

- What are the implications for Ministry of the Word and Sacraments of change in the life of the local church? How do we avoid pragmatic and piecemeal responses and ensure theological integrity as well as pastoral sensitivity?

FIVE

REFLECTION 4

WHERE ARE WE GOING?

NUMBERS

Numbers might indicate where we have come from and the journey over time so far, but cannot tell the whole story. They may not be reliable and relate to members and children and not to Ministry or Ministers, or discipleship, or mission, or faithful witness to and proclamation of the gospel. They depend on how well records are kept, how regularly they are updated and how the data is reported. The life of the local church might therefore be described in other terms, for example, in the range of weekday activity, in footfall, in intentional mission engagement.

Early records included the number of teachers alongside the number of children, but there is no record of the service of others, including elders, except perhaps in the minutes of church and elders' meetings. Nevertheless, here are some numbers from the Annual Returns that are of personal interest that provide a basis for comment and reflection which will be of wider interest and application.

Bexley United Reformed Church is the church in which I grew up, where I became a church member in 1974 and where the processes that led to my ordination began.

1973-74	163 members	118 children
1987-88	77 members	113 children
2019	48 members	35 children

Stoke United Reformed Church, Coventry is the church in which I was ordained in 1986. I was Minister there until 1991, with two part-time colleagues in a group of five churches.

1973-74	147 members	98 children
1987-88	93 members	36 children
2019	28 members	

The church is now amalgamated with Wyken United Reformed Church to form Ansty Road United Reformed Church on the Wyken site. The Stoke building has been sold.

I was inducted as Minister at **Pype Hayes United Reformed Church** in 1991 and served there part-time until the end of 2000, alongside Ministry in the Hodge Hill Local Ecumenical Partnership (LEP).

1973-74	142 members	81 children
1987-88	89 members	30 children
2019	23 members	

In September 2001 I was inducted as Minister in **St John's United Reformed Church, Stourbridge** to serve part-time alongside the Synod Lay Training Officer role. Scoping was reduced in 2005 when I was inducted to serve in addition as Minister in the United Church, Halesowen. I served as Minister in both churches until October 2016. St John's closed in January 2017.

1973-74	142 members	59 children
(on the original site in Lower High Street, Stourbridge)		
1987-88	115 members	70 children
(85 URC in a LEP with the Church of England, in the Anglican building)		
2019	Closed	

These numbers show a remarkably similar pattern across different social, geographical and ecclesiastical contexts. On the basis of statistics such as these, decisions have been made on Ministerial deployment. All these churches would at one time have been "single pastorates" served by their own Minister of the Word and Sacraments. The impact of this pattern on church membership is not clear, although there is some anecdotal evidence that numerical growth and renewal occurs when churches are provided with leadership from external sources beyond their own capacity or ability to support financially. This is part of the rationale of the provision of Special Category Ministry in the United Reformed Church.

These churches are now provided with Ministry in quite distinct ways. The flexibility and freedom given to Synods to develop their own pattern and practice has resulted in considerable diversity but also possibly confusion of roles and theological inconsistency. **Bexley** is now in a group pastorate with two other churches, in Bexleyheath and Welling. The **Stoke** Church was for a lengthy period part of the East Coventry Group (with four other United Reformed Churches) and also shared in a Local Ecumenical Covenant in the 1980s and 1990s. Ansty Road was for a period subsequently grouped with St Columba's United Reformed Church, previously part of another group pastorate, until St Columba's closed at the end of 2020. **Pype Hayes** has been led in recent years by an Elder in Local Leadership (the term the Synod has adopted for an increasing number of posts, developed largely ad hoc in response to local need and dependent on the availability of a suitable individual to provide leadership). The United Reformed Church in **Stourbridge** had united with St John's, Stourbridge in a Local Ecumenical Partnership in the 1970s for a period of over twenty-five years until the Partnership collapsed and the building was sold to the United Reformed Church by the Diocese of Worcester. Its Ministry however throughout that period was provided solely by the United Reformed Church.

In *Under God's Good Hand*, his 1998 history of the traditions which have come together in the United

Reformed Church, David Cornick[89] describes the United Reformed Church contribution to contours of church life in the late 1970s and 1980s, pointing out initially the contribution to attitudes to social affairs, and then the changing pattern of religious allegiance. Noting and giving specific detail of general decline, he observes variations with the general pattern and refers to Grace Davie's study.[90] The crisis facing the churches was not one of believing but belonging, which he sees reflected in the ratio of members to adherents in the United Reformed Church.

A sensitive future historian, he then writes, *may discover a third contour, that the United Reformed Church has remained faithful to its calling. It has continued to proclaim the gospel in innovative and creative ways, often in the hardest of places. The membership of the churches has declined, the number of churches has not.*

He provides these statistics in support:

	Members	Buildings	Ministers
1972	200,000	2080	1841
1995	102,000	1784	813
Reduction	49%	15%	56%

---

89 At the time of writing (July 2021) Fellow and Director of Studies in Theology and Religious Studies, Robinson College, Cambridge. Formerly Principal of Westminster College, Cambridge (1996-2001), General Secretary of the United Reformed Church (2001-2008) and General Secretary of Churches Together in England (2008-2018).

90 Davie, G. 1994.

Those figures may be interpreted in two ways, he then argues. *It may be seen as the inheritance of a Congregationalism whose demographic pattern throughout the century has included a large number of small churches. It can also be understood as a refusal to forsake the 'front line' of missionary engagement. There has been a determination, for example, to do all that is possible to maintain a presence in our inner cities, and the development of the ministry of Church Related Community Workers has been a significant, if small, witness to creative thinking about the relationship of church and community.*

This, he suggests is a consequence: *Maintaining the front line of mission with a falling ratio of members to churches has caused difficulties in providing ministry for all churches, and the denomination still struggles to find an appropriate pattern of ministry which is both responsive to its own needs yet also ecumenically responsible.*[91]

There is a common pattern of numerical decline, but considerable diversity in the steps that have then been taken in relation to the provision of Ministry. In some cases this has been provided through local initiative, while in others decisions made in Councils of the United Reformed Church have had significant impact locally. There is little evidence of consistency, coherence or strategic planning. The system in place has developed over time but decisions on deployment and scoping have largely been made at Synod level, and on an ad hoc and reactive basis. Current focus and action on deployment, rather than focussing on freeing up and enabling considered and effective use of a valued and essential

---

91   Cornick, D. 1998 pp.186-187.

resource, risks becoming an exercise in damage limitation, in which the powerful and articulate exercise undue influence, many feel powerless to address their own situation and important voices are not heard. There are of course no simple solutions to the current shortage of Ministers and I am not suggesting that the energy and time currently given to the focus on deployment is misplaced, but the limitations of the current system are clear.

In any case, it should be noted that the United Reformed Church does not in fact "deploy" its Ministers, but seeks to respond to call and invitation. However, in the current situation, there is little scope for movement, either in areas where there is deemed to be over-deployment or where under-deployment is common experience. Churches do not receive Ministry either because they are not permitted to call a Minister or are unable to attract a Minister to their particular location. At the same time, all contribute to the Ministry and Mission Fund. A financial commitment is made at Synod level to contribute to national funds and the Synods devise their own formula in seeking to share the burden equitably among churches.[92] I suggest again the potential for a thorough review, including an open and honest audit of all local church and Synod financial resources.

I suggest that within the United Reformed Church there is considerable expertise and experience which might open the way to new possibilities and patterns of Ministry but proper account needs to be taken of the costs and the

---

92 I am grateful to Robert Pope for drawing particular attention to this issue.

risks. The challenge remains to sustain traditional patterns of Church and Ministry while ensuring new patterns can develop with consistency and clarity in theology and practice. There is no one size fits all but gifts of Ministry to resource today's and tomorrow's Church to be the sign, instrument and foretaste of the kingdom of God need to be discerned and developed.

New ecclesial communities, new forms of church and Fresh Expressions may require new forms of Ministry but, holding to the Reformed tradition, will also require Ministry of the Word and Sacraments. An essential and urgent part of the task of review would be to discern the forms that such Ministry might take, in mutual accountability. As God's story in the human story unfolds in, among and through us as the people of God, we need vision and discernment in the exploration of how we get from where we are to where we might want to be.

Consistently proposals brought to General Assembly have recognised the need for flexibility but have been rejected or adopted in a stopgap and piecemeal rather than targeted and strategic manner. It may not be possible to forecast the extent and nature of social change and its impact on local communities and congregations, but when and where new patterns and forms of Ministry have been introduced there has often been little joined-up thinking and insufficient attention to the detail and the implications. I will describe and discuss some examples in Reflection 5 in which initiatives in mission are often dependent on local resources of buildings and finance, and local and wider co-operation which might be either ecumenical or from within the community, but alongside the particular and distinctive gifts of imagination and creativity of the Minister. A more strategic approach is needed with clear priorities if such initiatives are to result in consistent change.

PERSPECTIVES
DOUG GAY[93]

Gay describes the Church of Scotland, the Kirk, as facing particular pressure. To this point the Kirk has been able to continue to provide a Minister for each of its churches but this is no longer possible. Gay discusses four strategies in response: more candidates, fewer parishes, new forms of ordination, and greater flexibility in assignments. In respect to the latter, he suggests three new forms of Ministry: (1) a new form of commissioned rather than ordained eldership serving for a limited but renewable term of three years, (2) drawing from the practice in other Reformed Churches in the appointment of specific elders as "Commissioned Local Ministers", trained and authorised and potentially paid for Ministry including presidency at the Sacraments, and (3) the creation of part-time posts including house for duty. This is similar territory to that explored by the United Reformed Church and the response in the provision of NSM4.

I note that the polity of the Church of Scotland may look similar to the United Reformed Church but is in fact quite different. In Scottish Presbyterianism there is more central control and the structure and nature of authority enable decision-making at Presbytery or Assembly level.

93 Gay, D. 2017.

Nevertheless, it is not always possible for the Kirk to move swiftly or sensitively in response to the challenges Gay describes and explores.

Gay discusses some possible responses, in accordance with the condition of the local church; (1) closing the unviable; (2) managing the declining; (3) supporting the declining to grow; (4) supporting the growing; (5) planting new. The processes of discernment are key, but the detail can only be worked out on the ground, which presents a significant challenge. With the current level of resources of personnel and finance, it might not be possible to put all these responses into effect simultaneously and it is not clear who undertakes the vital and necessary task of assessing and deciding on priorities, and whether this should include consultation at a local level and in the wider Councils of the Church. On this last point my view is that the widest possible consultation is necessary. Gay also points out the importance of finance (he refers consistently, perhaps more emotively, to "money"). *Follow the money*, he writes. *If the money has not moved the power has not moved. If the power has not moved, we have not reformed the Kirk.*[94]

In other discussions, a traffic light system has been suggested to distinguish between levels of life and vitality in local churches:

Red – churches that have reached a standstill and are going nowhere

Red and amber – churches that are ready to move forward

---

94   Gay, D. 2017 p.97.

Green – churches that are moving forward

Amber – churches that are slowing down and preparing
to stop

Red

There are however issues about the management of such a system. It would be difficult to define criteria and to establish any degree of objectivity. The experience of St John's Church in Stourbridge suggests that it is at the local level that priorities for mission and Ministry should be discerned. In the life of the United Reformed Church, there are risks in decisions being taken by those claiming an objective and broader view while working from their own preconceptions and agendas.

TERRY HINKS

In the report on his 2017 sabbatical Terry Hinks, who has been a Minister in the United Reformed Church since 1986 and served in four pastorates, in Herefordshire, Hampshire and two in Berkshire and in two Synods, referred to isolation, individualism and resistance to teamwork amongst Ministers and encouraged the practice of appraisal and attention to accountability. In relation to the Church, he wrote *the challenge is to find a sustainable form of Church life, to identify and let go of the things we are no longer called to do and grasp what God is calling us to do and be, here and now.* [95]

Many would recognise this challenge; I suggest it is the consequences in practice that demand urgent attention. The rush to judgment on forms of church and the practice

---

95 Personal communication.

of discipleship must be avoided and loyal and faithful service acknowledged alongside suggestions for change. Sensitivity is needed; many will understand the service they have offered as their response to God's call on their lives and suggestion of change may appear threatening as well as judgmental.

DAVID PEEL

David Peel wrote, in 2012, *many of our churches are terminally ill and need Ministry to love them to death; others are being granted a future but want Ministry to enable them to make good use of their God-given gifts and opportunities; yet others are not sure where they are and require Ministry to help them read the signs of the times and discern their future one way or another.*[96] I point out that all these responses have been evident in the coronavirus pandemic. Some churches now recognise the opportunities that the "new normal" will present beyond the pandemic; some are determined to resume life as it was as far as is possible; others are struggling and fearful for the future. There is considerable uncertainty heightened by the isolation of lockdown. Yet placing churches into categories and making decisions on that basis remains problematic.

I suggest local churches can feel pressured into making decisions and need to be enabled and supported for honest and open conversations about their situation and possible scenarios without fear or threat, presumption, preconception or prejudice. Decisions should continue to be made at a local

---

96 Peel, D. 2012 p.110.

level as far as possible, with sympathetic advice and guidance available from the wider Church. A policy of euthanasia, even if supposedly voluntary, is not the only option. Death holds the potential for resurrection; winter holds the potential for spring growth.

DAVID THOMPSON[97]

David has been Convener of the Training Committee, is a former Moderator of General Assembly and served on a number of Assembly Working Parties and Review Groups. From a Churches of Christ background, he is also a Non-stipendiary Minister of the United Reformed Church. We discussed a number of key issues relating to the theology and practice of Ministry in the United Reformed Church.

The development of multiple pastorates has been taken for granted, although it is recognised that spreading Ministry increasingly thinly contributes to the burn out of Ministers and the frustration of local churches. Good practice requires attention to the management of expectations of Ministers and congregations and to time management.

The practice of closing churches is also taken for granted but often with no strategy, policy or plan in place beyond closure. It is commonly understood that the church meeting has the sole authority to close the church but it is too often the step of last resort when all else fails. Attention needs to be given to buildings, their location and use and to theologies of place and buildings. John Inge suggests church buildings

---

97 Reflections following a conversation at David's home 28th October 2019.

might be recognised, promoted and equipped as pilgrimage sites and holy places.[98]

Provision for Ministry formation and development in the United Reformed Church currently has three phases, Education for Ministry (EM) 1, 2 and 3. Reflective practice is now a key element in EM1. Beeley[99] and others describe "adaptive ministry". Alan Sell proposed a rigorous post-ordination programme.[100] The United Reformed Church continues to aspire to be a learning Church, but it is against the background of constraints of time and money and financial support for EM3 has been significantly reduced.[101] I suggest a more systematic approach to EM3 which would include the Resource Centres for Learning in planning and delivery would benefit Ministers and churches.

Training for elders has been consistently encouraged and materials revised but the role and responsibilities are in many places poorly understood and ineffectively practised. It is one of the areas in which the union with the Churches of Christ might have brought change, but the result was an influx of "auxiliary Ministers". This title was changed to Non-stipendiary Ministers and then Self-Supporting Ministers, but the resource has not been developed as originally envisaged and these Ministers can be seen as filling gaps, undervalued and ineffectively deployed.

It has been argued repeatedly that eldership is one of the

98   Inge, J. 2003.

99   Beeley, C. 2012.

100 Sell, A. P. F. 2016.

101 EM3 funding available was increased for 2021 to its previous level in response to the 2020 pandemic.

unique gifts of the United Reformed Church, particularly in relation to leadership and pastoral care. Yet the elders' meeting is often perceived as primarily concerned with management or as an executive body. The Churches of Christ model again might have provided a more consistent leadership similar to that undertaken by Elders in Local Leadership, but with clear responsibilities and accountability instead of the ad hoc and relatively haphazard current provision of those posts. The Churches of Christ also used the term "Evangelist". This role remains undervalued and poorly understood in the United Reformed Church.

In general, there has been a loss of any form of teaching Ministry even if it is expected and required by the local church. In many churches, the only time and place for teaching is the Sunday gathering for worship, dependent on the style and content of the lay preachers or worship leader and independent of the Ministry offered by the Minister of the Word and Sacraments. There is an inevitable loss of continuity and depth. Faith and discipleship might be nurtured within congregational life but an essential perspective must come from outside, in prayerful and communal study of the scriptures and in the wisdom gathered by and held in the tradition.

The introduction of pioneer Ministries brings important perspectives but should not be initiated independent of theology. More detailed and critical attention is needed to aims and objectives. There are particular initiatives in some Dioceses and from the Church Missionary Society (CMS). In the East Midlands region, the Ely Diocese has made a significant commitment to resource pioneer Ministry posts and the Eastern Synod has funded some innovative and imaginative forms of Ministry.

CMS is in the process of developing a number of hubs where training and equipping for diverse pioneer Ministries take place. This goes beyond the Fresh Expressions and Mission-shaped Ministry provision, but is generally a development of lay rather than ordained Ministry. Such Ministry might be seen as comparable with the congregational mission station of a century or so ago. Pioneer Ministries are also often time limited and contextual. Such Ministry requires particular gifts for a particular place at a particular time and it is not clear how this will work out on a large scale.[102]

The majority of United Reformed Churches would now be considered "small" churches and the large church with the potential to pay its own Minister, a practice not in any case permitted under the Plan for Partnership, is a rare exception. Attempts to define "small" are a distraction, although it should be noted that Carl Dudley has produced a new edition of his seminal 1978 book.[103] However, the shape of Ministry which has developed in the United Reformed Church does not and cannot now sustain the life of these small churches and enable them to be the sign, instrument and foretaste of the kingdom of God. In the present pattern, neither Ministers nor elders

---

102 There have been more recent developments. See United Reformed Church, 2022. *Newbigin Pioneering Hub.* [Online] Available at https://urc.org.uk/your-faith/more-about-ministry/newbigin-pioneering-hub/ [accessed 15th July 2022] and Church Mission Society, 2022. *Newbigin Pioneering Hub.* [Online] Available at https://pioneer.churchmissionsociety.org/newbigin-pioneering-hub/ [accessed 15th July 2022].

103 Dudley, C. S. 1978 and 2002.

can or should be expected to provide the vision and leadership that is needed and a new pattern must be developed, rooted in theology and practice, to energise, equip and enthuse the local church to offer worship, to build relationships, and respond to opportunities of witness and service in its local context.[104]

NEIL THOROGOOD[105]

I was grateful to have the opportunity to discuss current issues, challenges and changes relating to Ministry in the United Reformed Church with the Principal of Westminster College, Rev. Neil Thorogood.

Formation for Ministry (or Education for Ministry) in its initial phase (EM1) is currently recognised as exploration. A key objective is sustaining ordinands for the long term. In the first days of training at Westminster ordinands are presented with current pastorate profiles. They are faced with the reality of the likely contexts in which they will serve as Ministers, and practices are encouraged to maintain prayer and spirituality and to work collaboratively. It is recognised that all Ministry is collaborative and the training environment is a place to develop relationships. Training therefore takes place as far as possible with others in a "cohort" of peers and Ministers, recognising the need for Ministers to be protected from and take steps to guard themselves against unhealthy forms of isolation.[106]

---

104 The Baptist Union of Great Britain and Ireland 1984 Half the Denomination. London: The Baptist Union of Great Britain and Ireland although dated, presents some interesting conclusions.

105 Reflections from a conversation at Westminster College, Cambridge 5th November 2019.

106 I note that in 2020, General Assembly made pastoral supervision mandatory for all serving Ministers.

However, there is considerable variety and diversity both in churches and in Ministers. The majority of United Reformed Churches may be small but small churches can be resilient and the implications of the geographical location of churches should be given serious consideration. It is suggested the RCLs might be involved in deployment discussions. More generally, greater continuity between EM1, which takes place in the Resource Centre for Learning, and the practice of Ministry in the pastorate and the Synod would benefit Ministers and the churches in which they are called to serve.

The challenges relating to the training of Ministers and the transition from one phase of preparation for Ministry to another need to be addressed but there is space for experiment. One of the Synods has introduced the practice of calling Ministers to serve in "Missional partnerships". These "partnerships" have replaced "pastorates" but there is anecdotal evidence that at this early stage of their development there is no change to the perceived role and expectations of the Minister. I suggest there may be specific issues relating to the calling of a Minister to a "Missional partnership" within the Reformed tradition. In the Reformed tradition there is an understanding that the Minister is called by the people among whom and with whom they will serve. If the call is made on the basis of resources, this might be detrimental to the development of important pastoral relationships.

Attention needs to be given to the aspirations of Ministers and churches, and to strength-based initiatives such as "Appreciative Inquiry".[107] The polity of the United Reformed Church may make experiment easier than, for example, in the Church of England. As a result, there may be proportionally more examples of "Messy Church" initiatives in the United Reformed Church than in denominations with more hierarchical forms of government and less local freedom. Given local freedom however all United Reformed Church "Messy Church" initiatives may not adhere to the principles laid down by "Messy Church" as an organization and a brand.

The "Missional partnerships" initiative also demonstrates that reshaping promoted through denominational processes and structures does not always produce the expected response. The ethos of the partnerships is likely to be clearly understood in the specific Synod as rooted in missiological principles and generating life, but beyond the region, and particularly among Ministers, the partnerships risk being perceived as large and therefore unattractive pastorates and Ministry teams.

Non-stipendiary, local, ordained Ministry of the Word and Sacraments (NSM4) had recently been agreed by Mission Council and General Assembly and was in the process of being introduced. Response had been slow at the outset, but appeared to be gathering pace. The lack of initial response perhaps indicated that those already serving as Elders in Local Leadership might see further training as unnecessary, while others might consider training unnecessary if they perceive that those currently serving are perceived to be untrained.

---

107 https://urc.org.uk/latest-news/2310-appreciating-Church-book-and-website-launch.html [accessed 24th April 2020].

The underlying question remains "What are Ministers for?". There is need for clarity but also for development. It is not a matter of keeping the status quo or maintaining an established shape and pattern while the landscape changes. At the same time there are clearly understood core roles and functions, required gifts and aptitudes which are spelled out in the "Marks of Ministry of the Word and Sacraments" (see also Reflection 2). Expectations need to be managed and there is a particular need to educate the churches. In some cases, it might be a matter of simplifying, in others a matter of stopping, activity. We do not look back on a golden age of church life and seek to replicate it, but are always being carried forward on the tide of history in God's time and purposes.

CONCLUSION

There are significant challenges to the United Reformed Church in relation to its local churches and its theology and practice of Ministry. We might find ways to discern where a particular church is on the journey, but there are serious concerns around the exercise of that discernment, particularly as it will be on the basis of that discernment that decisions will be made about the form of Ministry that can and should be available to any particular context. Decisions on support and training also ensue from those decisions. These are vitally important matters for the health, well-being and resilience of Ministers and for the growth and renewal of local churches. There are urgent questions to address: What Ministry or other support might be available to a church? What factors should be taken into account in assessing the stage of its development – number of members, pattern of missional engagement, geographical location? For how long, and on what terms should Ministry be provided? What is available and accessible? How does the denomination equip and train particular Ministers for particular Ministries? How do we allow sufficient flexibility and diversity while maintaining order and orthodoxy?

On the one side there is the desire to keep to the established and tried and tested shape and practice of Ministry of the Word and Sacraments that we know, and on the other to follow trends that seem to be delivering results elsewhere. A third way might be possible, to build (or rebuild) the confidence of the local church in the gospel and in itself so that it might discern and develop its own leadership in its own context, with space for the development of pioneer and community Ministries with support and oversight Ministry from the wider Church. Local leadership or the oversight Ministry might be the place for the Minister of the Word and Sacraments, while in every local church, elders provide spiritual leadership, with a designated and trained senior or ruling elder where available.

Kate Compston offers a positive and prophetic vision of the local church. It is poetic and aspirational yet describes characteristics which affirm the church as a place of God's activity, not separate from but engaged with the world where God is also present and active. I suggest Ministry of the Word and Sacraments is necessary to inspire and sustain such churches as the sign, instrument and foretaste of the kingdom of God.

"I dream of a Church that joins in with God's laughing
as she rocks in her rapture enjoying her art:
she's glad of her world, in its risking and growing:
'tis the child she has borne and holds close to her heart.

I dream of a Church that joins in with God's weeping
as she crouches, weighed down by the sorrow she sees:
she cries for the hostile, the cold and no hoping,
for she bears in herself our despair and disease.

I dream of a Church that joins in with God's dancing
as she moves like the wind and the wave and the fire:
a Church that can pick up its skirts, pirouetting,
with the steps that can signal God's deepest desire.

I dream of a Church that joins in with God's loving
as she bends to embrace the unlovely and lost,
a Church that can free, by its sharing and daring,
the imprisoned and poor, and then shoulder the cost.

God, make us a Church that joins in with your living,
as you cherish and challenge, rein in and release,
a Church that is winsome, impassioned, inspiring:
lioness of your justice, and lamb of your peace."[108]

QUESTIONS FOR DISCUSSION

- Where and how should decisions on the deployment of Ministers be made? What are the key factors to be considered?
- How might the life of the local church be measured and assessed? What factors relating to context should be taken into consideration? Is it more important that there should be a presence in some places than in others?
- What is the impact of culture change (e.g. post-modernism, individualism, secularism) on the life of the local church and on the practice of Ministry?
- What is the balance in Ministry between apostolic, prophetic, pastoral, educational and evangelistic roles and tasks?

SIX

REFLECTION 5

PIONEER MINISTRY - THEOLOGY AND PRACTICE

INTRODUCTION

The human story is part of the divine story and the Church is to be the sign, instrument and foretaste of the kingdom of God. The work of God is eternal but human enterprise always runs out of years. Endings can bring the possibility and potential of new beginnings. If established forms of Church and Ministry are in serious and rapid decline in the United Kingdom,[109] there is movement and promise in the development and provision of pioneer Ministries and new ecclesial communities. I consider some initiatives below

---

109 As evidenced by the current (2021) and urgent discussions of Ministerial deployment in the United Reformed Church.

but suggest that there is, at least as yet, no consistency in provision or training for these forms of Ministry. In the United Reformed Church in particular, there have been only a handful of posts which have arisen through local circumstances, funded either as a "Special Category Ministry", or from the resources of individual Synods. In this regard, some Synods have significantly more resources at their disposal than others. A system of resource sharing has been established which seeks to level the playing field, but its effectiveness remains open to question.

Carefully constructed and worked for projects and goals are sometimes superseded and we learn to live with loss and an apparent absence of meaning. God works with human fallibility and even apparent failure and defeat. In the life of the Church, as in society, we live increasingly with provisionality rather than permanence, with flexibility rather than order, and with variety rather than uniformity and consistency. It is therefore important to find meaning and purpose through holding together theology and practice, past and present, experience and tradition, learning and piety.

Sadgrove refers to the effects of consumerism and new sexual freedoms, the mistrust of institution, the collapse of traditional patterns of family life, and the overriding importance attached to personal opinion and lifestyle choice.[110] Morale, he argues, is a spiritual as well as a systemic issue. *However pessimistic about the outlook for organised religion, however unsure the clergy are becoming about their*

---

110 Sadgrove, M. 2008 p.121.

role, the answer is not to be merely dutiful, or to think that seriousness is the same thing as solemnity.[111] Moreover, *the best antidote to despair is thankfulness* and support and review are *generic approaches to recovering joy.*

David Peel suggests that *when we have not enough Ministers to go round we invent new types to satisfy the churches' craving.*[112] He argues that instead we need to use and enhance the Ministry we have and particularly the eldership, who can be leaders in mission. The Church's Ministry and mission also need to be owned by the whole Church. Ordained Ministry might be understood as of the "*bene esse*" rather than the "*esse*", for the well-being rather than constitutive of the Church, but Robert Pope suggests that these terms do not sit comfortably in the Reformed understanding of the Church because they present the argument the wrong way round. "The Church is where Christ is present and Christ is present in the Word and Sacraments. Through this we are strengthened to continue Christ's mission (as ambassadors, workers, signs, symbols, glimpses of the kingdom, drawing others to the vision, seeking the good of all) in the world."[113]

There is a growing literature related to pioneer Ministry[114] and CMS also has a dedicated website[115] and a regular

---

111 Sadgrove, M. 2008 p.130.

112 Peel, D. 2007 p.197.

113 Personal communication.

114 Moynagh, M. 2012, 2014 and 2017, Moynagh, M. and Milne, A. 2016, Ross, C. and Baker, J. (ed.) 2014 and 2015, Ross, C. and Smith, C. (ed.) 2018.

115 https://pioneer.Churchmissionsociety.org/ [accessed 24th April 2020].

publication, *ANVIL*.[116] Janet Wootton has suggested that each generation feels like a pioneer. She argues that Ministry must be redefined in style and particularly in the light of the *failure of dominant cultures to recognise their inculturation of gospel and Church and their tendency to see their own view as simple, correct and normative*.[117] She suggests that responses to the complexity that marks today's culture might include shared Ministry with justice and liberation at the core, and fresh expressions not based in institution.

Jonny Baker describes the Church as an institution as *stuck in its yesterday*,[118] living within the consumer culture but resisting consumerism, seeking to be formed by the gospel. However, *Pioneers need to be formed and located in a prophetic community truly to sustain and nurture the mission spirituality required for this difficult task* and *part of the challenge is to embody the spirituality and posture of prophetic dialogue in relation to the wider Church – to be gentle among, listening and discerning what the Spirit is doing but also to be reforming Christian tradition in a prophetic Spirit, beckoning the Church into the future*.[119]

---

116 https://pioneer.Churchmissionsociety.org/ [accessed 24th April 2020].

117 Wootton, J. (ed.) 2007 p.89.

118 Ross, C. and Smith, C. (ed.) 2018 p.213.

119 Ross, C. and Smith, C. (ed.) 2018 p.214.

STORIES
CATHY ROSS, DIRECTOR FOR PIONEER
MINISTRY WITH CMS[120]

In December 2019, CMS had eighty lay students and twenty ordinands in training for pioneer Ministry at Cuddesdon College in Oxford. Courses were taught in evenings and at weekends at the Oxford centre and also at Roehampton University while other hubs had also been set up. In some cases, this was providing material for CME (Continuing Ministerial Education) for Church of England clergy, but the centre also offers courses through Common Awards validated by Durham University at undergraduate and postgraduate level.

Some Dioceses have embraced the need for pioneer Ministry but this is not evident across the Church of England and Ross suggested that training for all ordinands in aspects of pioneer Ministry might be an objective. There is funding available for clergy training through the Church Commissioners but lay people predominantly provide their own funding and there is little or no financial support available to them from Church sources. The relationship of the training provided through CMS to structures and training institutions more widely has yet to be addressed.

CMS is responding to specific demand and need. Teamwork and collaborative skills are key components in the training provided and it is not perceived as for the maverick or "lone ranger". Further, Ross stated that there is no one single model of pioneer Ministry. Michael Moynagh

---

120 Information from conversation with Cathy Ross, Director for Pioneer Ministry with CMS, at CMS Oxford 13th December 2019.

describes a spectrum from community development to church planting. Ross emphasised that the model is not the church-planting model of which Holy Trinity Brompton is an exemplar, although this model might be applicable to a small number of projects. Typical pioneer Ministries are contextual and bottom-up initiatives, and, although some are linked to parishes, the majority do not begin with a church, a building, a system or a structure. It appears to me that there has been little consideration of the relationship between pioneer Ministries and new ecclesial communities and previous church-planting models and strategies.

Funding is an issue in some contexts, with a related issue of termed contracts, and funding is often available for a limited term or linked to outcomes. There is evidence that for a project to become established long-term investment of time and gifts are necessary and an aim to become self-funding. At present this is an area of experiment and the importance of starting small is recognised. There are in any case a limited number of posts, many of which are starting from scratch, using the gifts and skills of those prepared to offer them in an experimental form of Ministry. Ross quoted two specific examples – a boxing club and a beauty salon.

Ross described the model of learning as "learning by doing" alongside reflective practice, in contrast to traditional models of theological training. Further, the practice of observation, which students undertake on placement in traditional patterns of training, is not encouraged. She argued action, targeted and intentionally missional activity, lead to acceptance in a local context, and the development of identification and belonging.

ANDREW DUNLOP, TUTOR IN CONTEXT-BASED TRAINING, RIDLEY HALL, CAMBRIDGE[121]

Dunlop has experience as an Anglican priest of pioneer Ministry in two different contexts and now teaches ordinands for pioneer Ministry at Ridley College, Cambridge. Key words in conversation with him were integration, collaboration, resourcing, continuity and strategy. He said there is so far no single approach in the Church of England in the establishment of posts. An initiative for pioneer Ministry may come from an individual, a context or a Diocese. Projects and Ministries begin in various ways through interaction between Diocesan Officers and those in contexts where a post is proposed.

Dunlop has published the stories and offered reflection on his experience in two different contexts, with Anna Brooke in the Grove booklet, *Mixed Economy Mission*,[122] and at greater length and depth and with extensive theological reflection in *Out of Nothing*.[123] In both cases the development of the project is relationship-based and community-focused. I suggest there are clear parallels with Church Related Community Work Ministry in the United Reformed Church.

In *Out of Nothing* Dunlop discusses theologies of atonement and reflects on what constitutes church. He refers to *participating in the atoning activity of God through ministry and the day-to-day lives of its members*[124] and it is this participation that gives the church validity. He discusses

---

121 Information and reflection from a conversation at Ridley College, Cambridge 21st November 2019.

122 Brooker, A. and Dunlop, A. 2019.

123 Dunlop, A. 2018.

124 Dunlop, A. 2018 p.127.

sustainability with reference to discipleship, leadership and finance. However, the focus is on relationship and individual journeys rather than structures and finance. He also suggests evaluating fruitfulness with reference to four directions of relationship – up with God, in with one another, out to the world, and of the wider Church – and considers appropriate fruit for each stage of development. He argues each of the four directions of relationship is broken and atonement is offered in Christ.

This is the primary action of God in Christ and Dunlop suggests the question that therefore needs to be addressed in relation to the fruitfulness of a new ecclesial community is *Are people being atoned?*, i.e. are broken relationships in each direction being healed and restored? He suggests that places of encounter are *atoning moments when God reaches out to us and draws us in to himself* and concludes, *If, as I have argued, the Church is to witness and participate in the action of God in Christ, we can therefore use the doctrine of atonement in our shaping of and evaluation of new ecclesial communities. This ensures that our Churches remain cross-shaped, focused on the essential work of God in the world. This approach is inherently relational and pays attention to the four directions of relationship that exist (up, in, with, of).*[125]

Dunlop argues that the key experiential elements – community, welcome, local, faith, identity, discipleship, attendance, involvement, worship, transformation, confidence, purpose – all demonstrate atonement in the four dimensions of relationship with God and with the world. Participation in

---

125 Dunlop, A. 2018 pp.135-6.

God's action is the focus of activity, providing and creating spaces for God to be experienced and recognised, enabling people to reach out to God from nothingness, weakness and human limitation. He suggests that this might also provide a basis for the evaluation of traditional Church.

Dunlop left one project after five years and reflecting on leaving draws on the experience of Oliver Donovan in the Masai culture. Donovan wrote, *The final missionary step as regards any nation or culture, and the most important lesson we will ever teach them, is to leave them.*[126] Dunlop says, *pioneers must move on to allow the gospel to be fully contextualised in the culture.*[127] He refers to the need for succession planning and the emergence of local leadership. It was important for him to leave a community that would continue the work, with a new ecclesial structure and a mixed economy in place. Leaving was difficult, but he felt called into a new role and able to leave the work in God's hands.

SIMON GODDARD, LEADER, RIVERTREE CENTRE FOR PIONEER LEADERSHIP

Simon Goddard is a Fresh Expressions missioner, a Baptist currently developing a pioneer school online. In online conversation he described and discussed a number of issues and elements relating to pioneer Ministry.[128]

He suggested an objective might be to embed pioneering within denominational structures but it is primarily a lay

---

126 Donovan, V. J. 1982 p.163.

127 Dunlop, A. 2018 p.149.

128 Information and reflection from online conversation 20th November 2019.

movement, equipping people where they are. Nevertheless, it might be included in ordination training. Across the documented spectrum of pioneer Ministry[129] home-grown leaders are engaged in teamworking providing continuity but also able to give time to networking. These processes are generally long term and the focus is on building the kingdom rather than the Church or establishing connections between Church and community. He also suggested regular review is needed which explores hopes and aspirations, and fruitfulness if not necessarily success in simplistic terms. Some initiatives might in any case be seasonal or short term.

In relation to denominational structures pioneers are usually on the edge.[130] There is a risk of encouraging "lone rangers" and maverick activity but a covenant relationship was suggested in which there are clear and high levels of accountability but low levels of control. Goddard claimed that appropriate attention is given to issues of sustainability, intentionality and purpose.

Key areas for learning and skills development might be reflective practice and change management but learning is

---

129 Hodgett, T. and Bradbury, P. ANVIL Vol. 34 Issue 1 no date.

130 As I have mentioned previously, George Lings' accounts of early pioneer work were published as Encounters on the Edge, a series of quarterly booklets from Church Army's Research Unit, exploring the wide range of Church plants and fresh expressions to come out of the Church of England. It ran from 1999 to 2012, reaching a total of fifty-six issues. The majority of the issues were based on case studies (most in the UK, but some international), reflecting on good practice, and including strategic and theological commentary. Other issues covered generic subjects related to fresh expressions of Church. https://churcharmy.org/our-work/research/publications/encounters-on-the-edge/ [accessed 29th March 2022].

by doing, on the job. The starting point is not the Church. The Ministry provided and the development of the project begin with vision and two important aspects are described as "just in case" and "just in time". Equipping then takes place on the journey rather than in elaborate, lengthy and detailed preparation. The emphasis is on paradigm rather than programme, and moving away from the role of Minister as permission giver. The Minister is not an obstacle, but released and enabled to work contextually and missionally.

RUTH MAXEY, MINISTER, CHURCH WITHOUT WALLS, MILTON KEYNES[131]

Ruth Maxey is a Minister of the United Reformed Church in a pioneer Ministry post in Milton Keynes, a United Reformed Church Special Category Ministry in Local Ecumenical Partnership with the Church of England. The Diocese provide the Rectory, where Ruth lives with her family and which is the base for much of the activity.

Ruth described her present post as having "come home". She offers some important reflection in her 2011 report[132] of her sabbatical experience in a previous post. She describes learning through experience and collaboratively and being "out of step". She refers to being not "under or over" but "in" scripture and reflects on the relationship between Church and culture. She recognises the importance of the worship space but also refers to "soft edges and a committed core" to her faith and life that is not rooted in institutional function.

---

131 Information and reflection from conversation at Ruth's manse 21st November 2019.

132 https://ruthmaxey.wordpress.com/ [accessed 26th November 2019].

She expresses a preference for "institutional fluidity" and "connection". She blogged, "I wanted a faith that changed lives, that transformed the world. I believed in a personal relationship with Jesus. I wanted worship that was emotional and passionate. I began to not want to live in two worlds, to bridge the cultural gap between my Christian life and the rest of my life."

We discussed leadership in the project and the issues of continuity both for the Minister and the project. Unusually perhaps for a pioneer Ministry project, the activity is already self-financing. The project gives scope for individuality, creativity and imagination but Ruth takes on the high levels of organisation that are required. The usual channels of decision-making in the United Reformed Church, through Councils and meetings, are sometimes subverted but Ruth seeks to avoid the emphasis on particular functions for Ministers which she perceives as marking much Church activity and might be seen to limit and constrain the Minister of the Word and Sacraments. She prefers and adopts a more pragmatic approach, doing whatever is necessary for an activity to take place.

The development of a variety of activity has been organic and focused on building relationships. Activity is people-centred but all under the title "Church without walls", in the absence of a building for regular use. There is some seasonal activity but elements of permanence as well as provisionality. An appropriate analogy might be the tree that passes through the seasons with different forms of activity in the different seasons but all maintain, develop and sustain growth and fruitfulness.

In relation to continuity, sustainability and succession Ruth emphasised local leadership and the importance of establishing roots and enabling connectedness, as well as encouraging participation which develops the sense of belonging and identity. Collaboration and depth of relationship are vital. She understands that the appointment of her successor, whenever that might be, will be key for the project. To this point she has offered gifts that in many ways are those of the Church Related Community Work Minister, but considers that administrative gifts might be particularly important for her successor. It was less clear how the particular gifts, skills and experience she brings to this role might be transferrable elsewhere in the United Reformed Church. There is little here that might be described as traditional or typical.

HELENE TAME, COMMUNITY CHAPLAIN, LOVES FARM, ST NEOTS[133]

Helene Tame is an ordained Anglican priest who was appointed to the United Reformed Church post on Loves Farm, St Neots, before she completed her ordination training in Oxford. The project is funded directly by the Eastern Synod of the United Reformed Church.

In conversation, she referred to community, encounter and discipleship as the key elements of her Ministry and life on Loves Farm. The project is not Church-centred, but "Breakfast Church" has developed which attracts fifty people

---

133 Information and reflection from conversation at Helene's home 26th November 2019.

and there is a "Messy Church" initiative. There is a focus on the Church "looking like Loves Farm", on belonging and diversity.

She has provided leadership with a team of three couples and established a presence on the estate. She holds a number of roles in the local community and refers to herself as "community chaplain". She played a key role in developing the Community Association, and a Community Centre is to be built in the near future. There is debt counselling and youth ministry and she has also developed a strong relationship with the local school. In contrast to Ruth Maxey's appointment, her post is open-ended and so, for the present at least, succession planning is not an issue.

JANET SUTTON WEBB, EVANGELISM COACH, CHANGING MARKET TOWNS PROJECT, DIOCESE OF ELY

Janet Sutton Webb[134] is currently employed by the Ely Diocese in a development role but claims to be the first pioneer Minister in the United Reformed Church, when she served in Okehampton in Devon. In conversation we discussed the principle of modelling and the deployment and training implications of pioneer Ministry particularly in light of the fact that pioneer Ministry is always for and in a specific context.

---

134 Information and reflection from conversation at the Punter, Cambridge October 2019.

THE ABERDEEN PRESBYTERY, CHURCH OF SCOTLAND

Doug Gay[135] wrote there is *no vision, skills or investment for planting* in the Church of Scotland but there have been more recent conversations with CMS.[136] Further, in October 2019 the Aberdeen Presbytery of the Church of Scotland released a report with radical proposals towards a sustainable future.[137] The plan has been widely reported, by the BBC,[138] *The Scotsman*,[139] and Premier.[140]

Speaking about the report, Planning Convener for the Presbytery, Rev. Scott Rennie said: "The Presbytery has a legacy of many more Church buildings than they need. We recognise that we will have to make some difficult choices on which buildings should be retained and which should be let go." He continued, "If the plan is followed through it will lead to significant new investment in Church communities across the city, as well as the formation of new worshipping communities in different kinds of spaces and buildings. The future for the Church of Scotland is to be closer to our communities, meeting in a range of different spaces, as well as investing in buildings which meet our needs now

---

135 Gay, D. 2017 p.91.

136 From conversation with Cathy Ross.

137 http://www.aberdeenpresbytery.org.uk/latest-news/presbytery-plan/ [accessed 12th March 2020].

138 https://www.bbc.co.uk/news/uk-scotland-north-east-orkney-shetland-49985067 [accessed 12th March 2020].

139 https://www.scotsman.com/news/almost-half-aberdeens-Churches-would-be-sold-under-major-Church-scotland-review-1405619 [accessed 12th March 2020].

140 https://premierchristian.news/en/news/article/Church-of-scotland-to-sell-half-its-aberdeen-Churches [accessed 12th March 2020].

and in the future. By coming together as lay people, and as Ministers serving our communities and city, to consider this issue we believe we can make a greater impact for the good of everyone." I point out the echoes here of the "Equipping the Saints" recommendations referred to in Reflection 2.

CONCLUSION

Fresh Expressions[141] take different forms but four features are described as key. These are (1) missional, for people who do not, or no longer, go to church; (2) contextual, taking seriously the culture in which they are set and neither imposing nor assuming a certain way of doing things; (3) formational, growing as disciples and as a community of disciples, called to Christlikeness as a community of disciples, formed in community, over time, through daily habits of obedience to God; and (4) ecclesial, seeking to establish churches, which may look different and seem different to what's been done before, but make discipleship a priority – valuing people's different faith journeys and supporting them as they wonder, explore and encounter.[142]

Before the Covid-19 pandemic the discussion of the future involvement of the United Reformed Church with the Fresh Expressions initiative included consideration of pioneer Ministry. These discussions continue. Peter Ball, Director of Church Resource Development at Westminster

141 Fresh Expressions, n.d. Fresh Expressions. [Online] Available at: https://freshexpressions.org.uk/ [accessed 24th April 2020].

142 https://freshexpressions.org.uk/about/what-is-a-fresh-expression/ [accessed 24th May 2021].

College, Cambridge, has also arranged a gathering of three people from a single church or project in each Synod involved in or with an interest in developing pioneer Ministries. They were meeting, prior to the pandemic, at Westminster College for three weekends a year and will resume meeting in due course. In addition, representatives from three Synods were meeting together to pursue a similar agenda of development and change and are also likely to resume activity. There has also been discussion of pioneer Ministry in the Committees and Councils of the United Reformed Church.

Through the discussions and the sharing of experience the potential is explored of whether and how new forms of Ministry might lead to the renewal of local United Reformed Churches. However, I suggest, there are two different dynamics.

Firstly, the response to reports to General Assembly as discussed in Reflection 3 indicates a preference in the churches for the continuity of established patterns of Ministry of the Word and Sacraments, in spite of the evidence that it is increasingly difficult to sustain. Change, including the introduction of Non-stipendiary Ministry, Church Related Community Work Ministry, Special Category Ministry posts and Elders in Local Leadership, has been against that background. The processes of call, selection, training and appointment for these forms of Ministry are well established, although there are persistent and pressing issues around the number of vocations and finance.

Secondly, and perhaps more significantly for the Church as institution and the denomination, pioneer Ministry is rooted and developed in a local context. It seeks to be "bottom up" rather than "top down" and frequently emerges as a result of action and commitment by those who are not ordained Ministers. As a result no consistent pattern for the development of pioneer Ministry has so far emerged from the stories and discussions to which I have referred.

In the institutional setting, clarity, cohesion and joined-up thinking are vital, particularly when resources are limited. In the United Reformed Church, the discussion of pioneer Ministry and new ecclesial communities presents various challenges to the shape and practice of Ministry of the Word and Sacraments. There is inevitably some tension between the traditional and the pioneer, the experimental and the established. Institutionally it might be fruitful therefore to explore and develop new models for oversight. Attention should be given to processes of decision-making and ways of encouraging attitudes and approaches which make it possible to stop, to let go, to simplify, or to be adventurous and take risks in responding to the leading of the Holy Spirit. There is an underlying issue of changing the mindset. When Ministry is seen and recognised in specific terms with set roles and functions there can be a significant barrier to experiment. At the same time, Churches' expectations of Ministry continue to be unrealistic.

Ways of encouraging freedom and flexibility are needed and, while presenting the potential of new opportunities, urgent attention must be given to discerning and discovering the real Ministry needs of the churches, as the churches themselves express them. Analysis and exploration are needed of the ways in which Ministers are currently deployed and when, where, whether and how different models might be developed. There is also an urgent task to educate the churches in the discernment, affirming and valuing of Ministry, and to develop the potential to recognise different models. Decisions must be made for the short term while developing a strategic approach for the whole of the United Reformed Church for the medium and longer term, which provides scope for creativity, flexibility and diversity and is realistic and achievable.

Pioneer Ministry must also be open to challenge and question. It might offer a way forward, but it remains the faithful giving of churches with a traditional pattern of life and Ministry which provides the majority of the financial support that makes experiment possible. "Traditional" churches need to be invited and encouraged to explore new possibilities, to be adventurous and to take risks while established ways of nurturing and sustaining faith are not threatened or undermined. I suggest that a mixed mode, with mutual understanding and support, might ensure that the gospel is handed on and the United Reformed Church does not run out of years.

There are challenges to be addressed in relation to the training and equipping of pioneer Ministers. It is important to remain open to the past, to learn and receive from it, holding for the present what is of value and passing it on for the future. Learning by doing has a place but might be questioned with regard to its effectiveness and appropriateness as the sole means of learning. Reflective practice is also important, but both learning by doing and reflective practice need to be balanced by scholarship to provide a secure and comprehensive theological basis for faith and practice.

Aspects of pioneering might be included in the training of all ordinands, in the same way as it is already, I am informed, in the "Stepwise" discipleship training resources.[143] The ownership and rooting of pioneering projects need to be considered and the resources they require, but there are risks as well as benefits in concentrating Ministry in a particular place against uncertain outcomes.

The current emphases on mission and discipleship in the United Reformed Church, though welcome, do not, I suggest, present potential for institutional change or in themselves lead to the renewal of the local church. A focus on numerical growth of the church also does not guarantee results. Attention needs to be focused on the tension between traditional and emerging church and to the issues of finance and support. The model offered by CMS, in which all Ministerial training is through the lens of mission, might offer an alternative training pathway.

Missiologically, however, we must guard against activity for its own sake. It is a commonplace that if anything can be mission then either everything is mission, or nothing is mission. Experiment must be subject to serious question and consideration. In Ross' terms, it may not be sufficient to ensure that activity is "targeted and intentionally missional". The activity also needs to be considered ecclesiologically. It should be underpinned by kingdom values – such as love, peace, justice, mercy, compassion, grace, and hope – individually and corporately. Fruitfulness might be evaluated on the basis of Dunlop's discussion of the doctrine of

143 https://urc.org.uk/stepwise.html [accessed 22nd May 2021].

atonement. Models of leadership in particular require more analysis.

Goddard's claim that appropriate attention is given to issues of sustainability, intentionality and purpose also merit further interrogation. Purpose is not always clearly defined. In some cases, the aim is the creation of a recognisable, worshipping, Christian community; in others action for change in the community is the focus; in yet others creating disciples may be seen as the primary objective.

There are particularly sharp challenges relating to buildings and finance. An initiative in one Diocese aims to have fifty per cent of clergy in pioneer roles within the medium term. This is a clear example of "following the money" to use Gay's terminology, although progress is as yet uncertain. The closure of churches may appear to be a solution but closing churches will not of itself result in renewal or advance the health and growth of other churches. Churches need to be offered support to reflect on their experience of decline in their own context, and to examine their expectations realistically and honestly, faithfully and hopefully. Closing churches in any case requires pastoral sensitivity, the provision of support and guidance and the opportunity to explore and inhabit processes of transition and change that might be life-giving. Further, it is essential to enable good endings, healthy grieving processes and ways of dealing with loss. The closure of a church does not guarantee a new beginning, or a new thing of any kind, but might open up new potential. In this respect, "Appreciative Inquiry", also referred to previously, may offer a valuable resource.

Some Synods are able to direct some of their own funds

towards pioneer Ministry. At this time, however, the impact of pioneer posts for Ministers and churches, for participants, for postholders and for communities remains unclear. The importance of sustainability needs to be both addressed and assessed. Key factors need to be determined in establishing a pioneer post or project alongside criteria of measurement of its "success" and fruitfulness, which would include details of timescale. Experiment needs both to be encouraged and yet is not always worthwhile or justifiable for its own sake. There might be reasonable expectations around continuity in relation to how far it is necessary, healthy or helpful for the project or for the pioneer. Consideration is essential of the capacity to develop any sort of experiment from an institutional perspective and what is necessary in terms of intentionality, particularly given that at present they often require significant resourcing from outside usual channels.

The relation between church and place and church and time might be helpfully, creatively and imaginatively explored and the recommendations of the "Equipping the Saints" report revisited in the light of Gay's proposals. We begin with what is and where we are, but what is and where we are should not define or constrain the life of the church and the coming of God's kingdom. Financial support for the Ministry of the Word and Sacraments and the deployment of Ministers of the Word and Sacraments is perhaps particularly important and significant at this time but I suggest a renewed emphasis on the shape and purpose of this Ministry is also timely, vital and central to the well-being of the Church and its potential health and growth. Balance and consistency in theology and practice are needed.

The churches and Councils, Committees and officers of the United Reformed Church face serious, deep and challenging questions going forward and there are very few simple or direct answers. This is a time for honesty, transparency and integrity as well as prayer and commitment in faith, hope and love across the whole of the denomination to ensure joined-up thinking and response.

QUESTIONS FOR DISCUSSION

- What from the past do you see as essential in the life of the Church today? What is negotiable?
- What is no longer valid?
- How might pioneering address the challenges and opportunities culture change brings to the Ministry of the Word and Sacraments?
- How far is it possible to hold pioneer Ministries and "traditional" Ministries together? How might it be achieved?

SEVEN

CONCLUSIONS

BEFORE THE COVID-19 PANDEMIC

THE IDENTITY AND PURPOSE OF THE CHURCH AND THE SHAPE OF MINISTRY

In 1965 Lesslie Newbigin wrote in the preface to *New Forms of Ministry* published for the World Council of Churches' Commission on World Mission and Evangelism: *What, in the new circumstances into which God has thrust us, is the pattern of ministry which is proper to the nature of the Church as God's apostolic community in this world?*[144]

We seek to provide leadership modelled on Christ himself, that is effective and productive, bearing fruit for the kingdom of God and for human flourishing for individuals and communities, for Church and world, and we look again to the Ministry of the Word and Sacraments but reframed and reshaped for a new age. Resources of time and money need to be directed to training for leadership, so that Ministry of the Word and Sacraments might

---

144 Paton, D. (ed.) 1965.

147

continue to be available as widely as possible. At the same time we need to be prepared to challenge and to explore with the churches different or new patterns of Ministry to sustain and nurture them for their health and growth and their engagement in God's mission in a new age.

In *The Open Secret*, Newbigin repeatedly described the Church as the *sign, instrument and foretaste of the kingdom of God.*[145] God is involved in mission, and sends the Church equipped and empowered for that mission. This is the secret that is open as God reveals himself through the Church he sent into the world. Moreover, the local church is the only hermeneutic of the gospel. He writes, *I have come to feel that the primary reality of which we have to take account in seeking for a Christian impact on public life is the Christian congregation. How is it possible that the gospel should be credible, that people should come to believe that the power which has the last word in human affairs is represented by a man hanging on a cross? I am suggesting that the only answer, the only hermeneutic of the gospel, is a congregation of men and women who believe it and live by it. I am, of course, not denying the importance of the many activities by which we seek to challenge public life with the gospel – evangelistic campaigns, distribution of Bibles and Christian literature, conferences, and even books such as this one. But I am saying that these are all secondary, and that they have power to accomplish their purpose only as they are rooted in and lead back to a believing community.*[146]

---

145 Newbigin, L. 1978 and 1995.
146 Newbigin, L. 1989 p.227.

David Peel suggested that it is missiology which shapes ecclesiology and ecclesiology which shapes Ministry. The Church is always primarily a "people's movement" and not "a tired institution". He suggests the heritage is best served when leaders have a key role in the transition from ways of being Church that are no longer viable to the discovery of new life and new ways of being Church.[147] He writes, *Responsible Church leaders today will need to act partly as ecclesial undertakers helping us to lay to rest dead ways of being Church, and thus enabling us to move on and discover new life. We will guard our heritage best though when our Church leaders also act as ecclesial midwives who help us to bring new ways of being Church into the world.*[148]

Church also, however, Peel argues, makes a difference by being the same, through appropriate contextualization and incarnational expression of the gospel, through affirmation, engagement, and learning. In the complexity of contemporary cultures, and recognising the pendulum swing of mission strategies, there is a need for "living tradition" while avoiding "dead traditionalism". We recognise some of the givens of where and who we are since *Church history shows how very difficult it is for an institutional Church to live by the gospel it preaches, dying to itself in order to live to God for others.*[149]

The Church must maintain its identity and establish its credibility, bridging biblical culture and contemporary culture. The management consultant Peter Drucker said, "culture eats strategy for breakfast". Gay develops the idea

---

147 Peel, D. 2006 p.95.
148 Peel, D. 2006 p.95.
149 Peel, D. 2006 p.98.

that culture might also "float" strategy.[150] The question "how?" must be central to the response and the key issues might be around leadership. We need to explore the nature of leadership the Church needs to respond to today's challenges in the life of Church and society and how the United Reformed Church might travel light and be swift of foot in an age of rapid change, while holding to its identity and purpose in its theology and practice.

The realities are clear, but the question that Newbigin asked more than half a century ago remains pertinent. Peel referred to an age of dying churches, of challenges to resource new initiatives, of stresses relating to structures which impact the local church, of diversity, of charismatic and prophetic individuals, of impressive Ministers, of deployment policies, and of burnout. We continue to seek a pattern of Ministry appropriate to new circumstances and, in Newbigin's words, *proper to the nature of the Church as God's apostolic community in this world.*

Peel also argued that consistency is a fundamental task at the interface of tradition and context. He suggested the root problems are spiritual and theological, rather than structural or related to resources. The primary task is to discern priorities as individuals, as congregations, as a denomination.

There are implications for the future shape of Ministry in the United Reformed Church. There is no single pattern of Ministry evident in the New Testament and in the early Church, although the fivefold model described in Ephesians 4:11, namely. *The gifts he gave were that some would be apostles, some prophets, some evangelists, some pastors and*

---

150 Gay, D. 2019.

teachers (Ephesians 4:11, *NRSV*), might provide a framework. The present diverse pattern – Stipendiary Ministers of the Word and Sacraments, Non-stipendiary Ministry in four different models, Church Related Community Work Ministry, Elders in Local Leadership – has developed over time. It is not clear how that pattern might be mapped onto the Ephesians 4 framework and it should be noted that the Reformed tradition has in any case held that apostles, prophets and evangelists belonged to the early Church but might re-emerge if circumstances require it.[151]

I suggest these key elements require consideration in shaping the Ministry of the Word and Sacraments: leadership, eldership, calling, vocation, collaboration and communication. The "Patterns of Ministry" proposals from a generation ago, rejected by the General Assembly, might be revisited to develop a model of leadership that is collegial and collaborative, communal and personal. The time may be right to reconsider those proposals and offer them as a basis for present and future action.

In *Ministry for Mission,* David Peel wrote, *Whatever 'professional' Ministry we have needs deploying to ensure that congregations flourish, while our Church Councils exist to serve congregations and equip them to their essential missionary work.*[152] Resources for Ministry and mission may be stretched almost to breaking point, and churches struggle to survive and live without hope. The churches' expectations of Ministry cannot be met by the denomination. In this

---

151 Calvin, J. 1960 IV iii 4. I am grateful to Robert Pope for this point.
152 Peel, D. 2003 p.73.

light, churches need to rediscover the gospel – their life as a local congregation is its only hermeneutic – and build relationships of integrity rooted in faith, hope and love. When all around speaks of death and decline, relationship is key to rediscovering the reality of resurrection.

In some cases, local churches and denominational structures may be running out of years, but we trust that God will continue to renew his Church, that the fire will continue to burn. There is potential in the exploration of the capacity for local forms of leadership that will be coherent, consistent and effective. In maintaining consistency and coherence the centre can impact the edge, and encourage new beginnings, experiment and imagination, and the renewal of local churches. New ways of being the apostolic community in the world are open for discovery and development.

We live in today's Church in a mixed economy, with the new and the old, with tradition and innovation, with a variety of provision and models. We prepare for tomorrow's Ministry, the flexibility and variety that marks much current practice. We return to the two crucial questions: What is the nature of Ministry that the Church needs? How are we going to provide it?

New models need not supplant old models but both should deepen the values that we already hold as gospel and kingdom values. Pickard refers to the *urgent need for collaborative and mutually enriching Ministries, interweaving spontaneity and stability, open to new expressions and resilient through creative adaptation.*[153] Later he describes Ministry as

---

153 Pickard, S. 2009 p.116.

not steady state but the *creative response to disturbance and information.*[154] I suggest there is time and place both for tradition and for experiment and for established and pioneer forms of Church and Ministry.

There has been a particular emphasis in recent times on Ministry as enabling and leadership as servant leadership. There is a considerable literature developed from the work of Robert K. Greenleaf who, it is claimed, coined the term "servant leader" in a 1970 essay. Greenleaf wrote, *The servant-leader is servant first... It begins with the natural feeling that one wants to serve, to serve first. Then conscious choice brings one to aspire to lead.* He continues, *A servant-leader focuses primarily on the growth and well-being of people and the communities to which they belong. While traditional leadership generally involves the accumulation and exercise of power by one at the "top of the pyramid", servant leadership is different. The servant-leader shares power, puts the needs of others first and helps people develop and perform as highly as possible.*[155]

This model of leadership is seen in Jesus and has consequently been applied to leadership in the Church. It may however be questioned if this is the focus of Christian Ministry, which is not serving others but serving God and responding to God's call in Christ, sharing the good news of new life and fulness of life in God's gift of himself. Effectiveness is not the only key to sustainability nor the necessary hallmark of faithful discipleship. A popular hymn

---

154 Pickard, S. 2009 p.143.

155 https://www.greenleaf.org/what-is-servant-leadership/ [accessed 24th May 2021]. See also Greenleaf, R. 2002 and Greenleaf, R. 2003.

at services of ordination and induction is "Brother, sister, let me serve you" but it includes these vital words: "*let me be* as Christ *to you*".

As W. H. Vanstone writes:

"Morning glory, starlit sky,
soaring music, scholar's truth,
flight of swallows, autumn leaves,
memory's treasure, grace of youth:

Open are the gifts of God,
gifts of love to mind and sense;
hidden is love's agony,
love's endeavor, love's expense.

Love that gives, gives ever more,
gives with zeal, with eager hands,
spares not, keeps not, all outpours,
ventures all its all expends.

Drained is love in making full,
bound in setting others free,
poor in making many rich,
weak in giving power to be.

Therefore he who shows us God
helpless hangs upon the tree;
and the nails and crown of thorns
tell of what God's love must be.

Here is God: no monarch he,
throned in easy state to reign;
here is God, whose arms of love
aching, spent, the world sustain."[156]

The effectiveness of Ministry cannot be measured in simple terms and against simple criteria, particularly of size and strength. There is strength in weakness: in God's economy of grace the small church has its place. The consequences of responding to God's calling are not necessarily the exponential growth of the church but the nurture and equipping of disciples and the enabling of response to God's Word, which the Ministry of the Word and Sacraments makes possible wherever people are, encouraging one another and building one another up until all attain the maturity that is God's will and purpose, *the measure of the full stature of Christ* (Ephesians 4:13, *NRSV*). Ministry of the Word and Sacraments is then rooted in relationship, the offering of the self, living out God's call, sharing the gospel in community without seeking recompense or reward. God's call is to faithfulness as well as fruitfulness.[157]

Ministers offer *collegial* leadership in representing the wider Church to the local, as well as the local to the wider

---

156 W.H. Vanstone (1923–1999) © reproduced by permission. Published by Darton, Longman and Todd 1977.

157 Thanks to Robert Pope for the reminder of this counter. My 2006 unpublished thesis "Redefining Small Churches – exploring issues of survival and change" argued that small churches have the potential to nurture and sustain faithful discipleship, witness and service in response to their own context and gifts and should be encouraged, supported and resourced to do so.

Church. The primary role of Ministers in the local church is as teachers and trainers, theologians and reflective practitioners, equipped and trained to share their knowledge, experience and expertise with local churches, giving oversight but also discerning and developing the gifts of others. They model leadership so that others might respond to God's call.

Ministers are resourced for their roles and responsibilities and for the relationships in which they serve through the Resource Centres for Learning which have a role in the management of change and should be included in processes of consultation. We can risk radical re-thinking of the functions of and gifts and preparation for Ministry but such thinking needs to be rooted theologically.

Ministers of the Word and Sacraments develop, train and equip elders to provide local, contextual leadership. I suggest that much of the future of the United Reformed Church might depend on an eldership that is properly supported and sustained but also challenged to its calling to leadership more seriously.[158]

The Basis of Union defines the functions of the elders' meeting: these are the first three: (i) to foster in the congregation concern for witness and service to the community, evangelism at home and abroad, Christian education, ecumenical action, local inter-Church relations and the wider responsibilities of the whole Church; (ii) to see that public worship is regularly offered and the Sacraments are duly administered, and generally to promote the

---

158 On the issues of leadership, see also Heifetz, R. 2000, Heifetz, R. 2009 and Heifetz, R. and Linsky, M. 2017.

welfare of the congregation; (iii) to ensure pastoral care of the congregation, in which the Minister is joined by elders having particular responsibility for groups of members.[159]

These functions of the elders' meeting demonstrate the *communal* dimension of leadership of the local church. Elders are called and elected by the local church. They are committed to the life of the local church and need to be trained, resourced and equipped consistently, not primarily to fulfil functions but to use their gifts to provide spiritual leadership and pastoral care, developing life-giving relationships. Elders also carry the vision of the local church and lead God's people in engagement in God's mission in the communities in which they are set. Consistent training should be provided through the Ministers, as well as from Synod and the RCLs. Greater consistency in challenging and equipping elders will provide both pastoral care in each and every context and the leadership that enables the local response relevant in each place and time. In local churches where elders provide passionate and imaginative leadership as well as faith, hope and love the church develops and lives out its mission as the sign, instrument and foretaste of the kingdom of God.

The denomination responds institutionally in the face of diminishing resources of people, finance and capital, to the need of the Church for leadership to respond to contemporary challenges and to hold to the tradition, the foundations of theology and practice on which its life rests.

---

159 https://urc.org.uk/images/the_manual/B-The_Manual_-_Section_B-2019.pdf p.4 [accessed 19th March 2021].

Co-ordination and consistency are vital, but there is no easy route to balance and clarity in the way forward. There is no viewpoint from which to offer an objective and unbiased view. A factor in current deployment discussions is that there are many views on the way forward to resolve the apparent crisis and no clear consensus. Meanwhile as time passes, decisions have to be made, as churches and structures and institutions may all be running out of years. I suggest there is an underlying necessity to recover the churches' confidence in the gospel and we will not do that if we do not hear local voices.

The question "How do we get from where we are now to where we might want to be?" (while recognising that is also a provisional place) needs to be addressed to local churches. Institutions and Councils sometimes appear to be conservative and reactionary, and to constrain rather than liberate. How do we listen afresh to what the Spirit is saying to the churches and allow the Spirit to move in local churches to rebuild hope and confidence? United Reformed Churches are being encouraged to "Walk the Way", "living the life of Jesus today".[160] We respond as individuals and together and whether gathered or dispersed to the challenges of discipleship, living and learning as bearers of the good news of God's love, peace and justice for individuals, communities and nations, but we need one another. The simplification of structures and the reduction or elimination of some institutional aspects of Church will help us travel

---

160 https://urc.org.uk/our-work/walking-the-way.html [accessed 24th April 2020].

light, be light on our feet and offer scope for creativity and imagination as we journey together.

Decisions have to be made about the use of resources. I suggest urgent attention to vocation, and the discernment and development of gifts for mission, Ministry, worship and service. The approach must be strategic and focused, taking into account the two clearly distinct but related directions of travel – towards pioneer Ministries and new ecclesial communities, nurturing faith and discipleship in new ways, and the equally important need for those who will continue to sustain congregational life in established ways through the preaching of the Word and the celebration of the Sacraments.

The two belong together. Is it possible to square the circle of disparate and even conflicting demands and expectation? Some emphasise that Ministry is for mission, with implications for church growth and development and change, and suggest all Ministry is pioneering. The churches and in particular the Councils of the Church however have repeatedly made it clear that the need they perceive is for more Ministers in the traditional model in which worship underpins the life of the church and sustains its witness and service and the priorities for Ministry are training in preaching and pastoral care, in theology and the Bible.

I suggest support and encouragement, time and money need to be invested to create new opportunities for individuals to respond to God's call to serve in both directions. The answers however do not lie with the Ministers or with the Councils but with the churches. Congregational life, elders' meetings and church meetings all need continual refreshment. The potential for meetings to be exciting, spiritual, life-giving opportunities for service needs to be unlocked. Meetings and those who share in them are not an organisational and institutional necessity, a means to an end, but contribute to the life and health, even the growth of the local church and the coming of the kingdom of God. Attention is needed to how Ministers, elders and others work together, supporting, strengthening and learning from one another in healthy, life-giving good news relationships.

We begin where we are, with diminishing numbers of members and Ministers, reducing financial resources and a loss of capacity and confidence. The buildings which are the focus for much of our activity in worship, mission and service are in many places no longer fit for purpose and beyond our capacity to maintain and develop. There are, however, ways of providing leadership to local churches which build confidence. They are rooted in collaboration, in teamwork and in shared leadership, and focus on people and relationships, listening to one another, discerning and developing vocation.

In the face of the apparent reluctance to address today's challenges and accept new shapes and patterns, it can be helpful to remind ourselves that in many ways the challenges are not new. Over time there is change. Ministry in the United Reformed Church has evolved and new forms have been developed, even if change has not been consistent, coherent or strategic. As we address today's and tomorrow's pressing issues, and consider the use and the expense of the expertise and experience of those who are trained and resourced in particular ways for particular tasks, we renew attention to the discernment of calling and vocation across the whole

Church. The calling to lead the Church in today's fast-changing world is in any context a call to risk, to adventure, to experiment, but it is, in W. H. Vanstone's phrase, *love's endeavour, love's expense.*[161]

The call to the Ministry of the Word and Sacraments persists; people still hear that call and respond to it, offering themselves in serving the faithful God. It is God who declares *I am about to do a new thing; now it springs forth, do you not perceive it? I will make a way in the wilderness and rivers in the desert* (Isaiah 43:19, NRSV). It is God who pours out new wine: *Neither is new wine put into old wineskins; otherwise, the skins burst, and the wine is spilled, and the skins are destroyed; but new wine is put into fresh wineskins, and so both are preserved* (Matthew 9:17, NRSV). The word of God is *living and active, sharper than any two-edged sword, piercing until it divides soul from spirit, joints from marrow; it is able to judge the thoughts and intentions of the heart* (Hebrews 4.12, NRSV) and, in response to faith, God calls into being that which does not yet exist: *it depends on faith, in order that the promise may rest on grace and be guaranteed to all his descendants, not only to the adherents of the law but also to those who share the faith of Abraham (for he is the father of all of us, as it is written, 'I have made you the father of many nations') – in the presence of the God in whom he believed, who gives life to the dead and calls into existence the things that do not exist* (Romans 4:16-17, NRSV).

There is no quick fix; there are no instant solutions. Mark Oakley, reflecting on the poetry of George Herbert, writes,

---

161 Vanstone, W. H. 1977.

The ego is the part of us that loves the status quo, even when it isn't working, and attaches our identity to the past and present, fearing the future.[162] We need to be honest and realistic about who we are and where we are while seeking a clear vision of who and where we want to be. Then together we might plan strategically not to maintain the institution as it is, but to take the necessary steps and initiate the necessary changes that take us into a future rooted in faith, hope and love for the coming of God's kingdom, of which we are the sign, instrument and foretaste. We look beyond ourselves to the God who is at work in us, among us and through us. In time we will all run out of years but for the moment we are on the journey, not always perhaps where we want to be or where God would have us be, but we celebrate God's continuing presence and blessing for the present and for the journey ahead. The fire goes on burning, as we continue in our searching and our dreaming.

R. S. Thomas writes in "The Bright Field",

"I have seen the sun break through
to illuminate a small field
for a while, and gone my way
and forgotten it. But that was the
pearl of great price, the one field that had
treasure in it. I realise now
that I must give all that I have
to possess it. Life is not hurrying

---

162 Oakley, M. 2019 p.6.

on to a receding future, nor hankering after
an imagined past. It is the turning
aside like Moses to the miracle
of the lit bush, to a brightness
that seemed as transitory as your youth
once, but is the eternity that awaits you."[163]

---

163 The Bright Field, R. S. Thomas in Percy, M. with others, 2014. ©
Orion Publishing Group Limited. Reproduced with permission of the
Licensor through PLSclear.

QUESTIONS FOR DISCUSSION

- Do you find it easier to relate to the Church as institution or as movement?
- What do you see as the negative and positive aspects of institution? And of movement?
- Has the model of Ministry in theology and practice changed dramatically? How do we hold together the nature of God and our participation in God's life in the world?
- What determines the shape of the Church and what it means to be Church? Does it follow from how we understand the nature of God as Trinity or from our understanding of mission?
- Have we lost sight and sense of God's presence among us? How might it be recovered?
- What might the renewal of the Church look like? What are the implications for worship? For mission? For discipleship?

EIGHT

REFLECTION 6

MINISTRY IN THE COVID-19 PANDEMIC

INTRODUCTION

Where to begin and, in due course, where to end? I began
these reflections with the story of Ministry and mission at St
John's United Reformed Church, Stourbridge from 2001 to
2016. It was a narrative of closure, of a local church running
out of years and an account of how events impacted me
personally.

This reflection is also rooted in personal experience but
the context is very different in two respects. Firstly, the initial
reflection marked closure in very specific ways, and there
had been the opportunity to process that experience over
a number of years. In contrast, this reflection on Ministry
during the Covid-19 pandemic has been written while the
pandemic is ongoing. It was originally written towards the end

of November 2020, revised in March 2021, and further revised in May 2021 and is based on information and experience at that time, although this final version was adapted and prepared for the purposes of publication in March 2022.

On 23rd March 2020 the first of a series of lockdowns in the United Kingdom had been announced. The first approved Covid-19 vaccine was deployed on 8th December 2020 but the apparently successful roll-out of the vaccination programme resulted in tensions between the advice of scientists and the actions of politicians which were not quickly resolved. In March 2022 legal restrictions, including the wearing of masks on public transport, in shops and other public places, limitations on travel, and the requirements of social distancing and self-isolation, were ended across the United Kingdom but guidelines continued to be in place. In the United Reformed Church the Moderators continued to encourage and advise caution.

Even with the ending of legal restrictions, there was still little sense of closure and no sign of an end to the impact of the virus, nor was there likely to be in the foreseeable future. The lasting impact could not be ascertained. Life might begin to return to normal, but could never be the same again. The discovery of effective vaccination had promised a way out but it was now known that the Covid-19 virus infection would continue and would need to be lived with, in the same way as flu, as it was increasingly said.

Secondly, the St John's, Stourbridge experience was shared with a relatively small group of people, particularly the congregation of St John's and partners in the local community. In contrast, the impact of Covid-19 is total. It impacts every individual and every community indiscriminately at every level on an unprecedented and global scale: every individual, group, community, society, nation: every organisation and business, industry and commerce, education and health (mental and physical), employment and economy. Moreover, the full extent of the impact cannot yet be predicted – politically, economically, educationally, socially, psychologically, spiritually and in relation to health, wealth and well-being for individuals, communities and nations.

Therefore I suggest that this is neither the place nor time for a detailed analysis of the impact of the pandemic on Ministry in the United Reformed Church. The time will come when we will be able to look back but for the moment the experience of the pandemic continues to be very real. This reflection is offered in *medias res*, without the benefit of hindsight or more mature reflection. However, I seek to offer some insights and reflection on the practice of Ministry in these complex and changing times.

PERSONAL PERSPECTIVE

T. S. Eliot reflects on place and time in his poem "Ash Wednesday":

"Because I do not hope to turn again
Because I do not hope
Because I do not hope to turn
Desiring this man's gift and that man's scope
I no longer strive to strive towards such things
(Why should the agèd eagle stretch its wings?)
Why should I mourn

The vanished power of the usual reign?
Because I do not hope to know again
The infirm glory of the positive hour
Because I do not think
Because I know I shall not know
The one veritable transitory power
Because I cannot drink
There, where trees flower, and springs flow, for there is
nothing again
Because I know that time is always time
And place is always and only place
And what is actual is actual only for one time
And only for one place
I rejoice that things are as they are and
I renounce the blessèd face
And renounce the voice
Because I cannot hope to turn again
Consequently I rejoice, having to construct something
Upon which to rejoice
And pray to God to have mercy upon us
And pray that I may forget
These matters that with myself I too much discuss
Too much explain
Because I do not hope to turn again
Let these words answer
For what is done, not to be done again
May the judgement not be too heavy upon us
Because these wings are no longer wings to fly
But merely vans to beat the air
The air which is now thoroughly small and dry

Smaller and dryer than the will
Teach us to care and not to care
Teach us to sit still.
Pray for us sinners now and at the hour of our death
Pray for us now and at the hour of our death."[164]

We have never done it this way before. The onset of the coronavirus pandemic in the spring of 2020 challenged the nation and its leaders and brought particular challenges to those in Ministry in the United Reformed Church.

My own story of the pandemic begins on 29th June 2019. On that day, my daughter and her fiancé were married at the Tabernacle United Reformed Church, Mumbles, Swansea and I was privileged to conduct the marriage service. In early December we gathered as a family for an early Christmas celebration and a few days later my daughter and her husband flew out to Tokyo, Japan for a late and extended honeymoon, returning from Singapore in mid-February 2020.

They are both experienced travellers (their wedding theme had been "the greatest adventure yet") and on honeymoon they travelled around the Far East, visiting Japan, South Korea, Thailand, Laos, Cambodia, Vietnam, Taiwan and Malaysia before their return from Singapore. During those months we traced their movements, and the progress of Covid-19, the pandemic which had started in Wuhan in mainland China and then almost seemed to pursue them as they travelled. They remained one jump ahead of the virus and returned home to Wales without drama.

---

164 Eliot, T. S. 2002. Reproduced with permission of the publisher.

When the pandemic took effect in the United Kingdom in March 2020, and the governments of Wales and Scotland set their own paths and restrictions, those living in Wales were allowed to travel no further than five miles from home, and there was no access across borders into Wales. As the couple settled back into home and domestic life parents on both sides, in England and Ireland, were unable to visit. Furthermore, when they were ready in mid-2020 to announce that Rebecca was expecting a baby, which in "normal" times would have been shared face to face, the news was shared in "Zoom" meetings, which by then were playing a significant part in the Ministry of Ministers serving in local churches and in other roles.

The political, social and economic landscape was changing fast and radically and has continued to do so. The Government frequently introduced new legislation, sometimes resulting in confusion and uncertainty for individuals, families and churches. As Rebecca and Eugene prepared for parenthood, we sought to offer appropriate support while not knowing what constraints on meeting there might be in the short, medium or longer term.

The experience of dislocation was shared by my son and his partner. They were living more locally to us, in rented accommodation in Solihull in the West Midlands, and used the opportunities of the lockdown and their six-week summer break as teachers to purchase their own property. They both continued to work through the lockdown and there were opportunities to meet with them through the different sets of legislation, with the required social distancing.

There is a further important aspect of this personal story. As the virus spread in the middle of March 2020 I fell ill, with some symptoms of the virus. The initial impact was brief but it was some time before I felt fit enough to return to work and I have continued to experience relatively minor health issues which may be related to Covid-19. A test in July 2020 was negative and I have no diagnosis but continue to undergo other tests.

My recovery from the illness took place at the same time as adapting to the new circumstances of "lockdown". It proved relatively simple for me to adapt to meetings on the "Zoom" platform but there were other implications and changes to the content and the pattern of the Ministry I exercise. Initially I shared the experience of isolation and disorientation but gradually new opportunities have emerged in consultation with colleagues within the Synod, the United Reformed Church and within the region ecumenically.

An early response was a Synod Ministers' conference "at home", which was well supported and generally well received. It was in many ways experimental and required considerable time and energy to prepare, but a great deal was learned about effective use of the software and it was possible to share resources and enable discussion.

Subsequently Ministers in the Synod have had regular opportunities to meet to share experience, and there have been similar opportunities for lay preachers which they have found particularly beneficial. These meetings have also been valuable in the development of my own role and responsibilities, providing opportunities to learn of the challenges faced by Ministers and churches as well as the variety of worship now being offered.

The value and importance of networking became clear. Networking offers support and encouragement and also enables the sharing of expertise and good practice, and avoids unnecessary duplication. Continued online meeting has considerable potential in that respect. It is necessary neither to travel long distances nor to meet for extended periods of time to justify the travelling time. It also offers some welcome relief from the experience of dislocation and desk-based boredom.

The impact of Covid-19 is unprecedented in our experience. Ministry has been exercised against the background of challenge and constraint. We have lived through extraordinary grief and loss which continue. The focus on worship and the care and compassion expressed in pastoral care have been and will remain important and essential. Internal concerns, and those of good order and government, are held in balance with the call to be prophetic and to make disciples while political, economic, social and technological realities shape the lives of individuals and communities. Ministers have responded with imagination, creativity, commitment and energy, but there is also a cost, which is yet to be fully borne.

There is a risk that the initial heroic response will be followed by disillusionment. Supportive and responsive networking might counter such a reaction. Communication has been key, when confusion and lack of clarity have frequently resulted from official government announcements. In the United Reformed Church, the Synod Moderators have provided clear leadership and informed and considered guidance. In the churches there are persisting fears and uncertainties, an awareness of weakness and vulnerability, and a perceived lack of capacity and resources, but it has been possible to hold on to hope and the potential of the "new normal", which will need to continue into the next phase and beyond.

PUBLISHED RESOURCES

Government legislation over the lockdown defined the parameters and created limits for activity. The wider Church has produced a range of resources providing information and guidance for local churches and Ministers. There has been an understandable focus on practical aspects, and particularly the use of buildings. Content and timing have been key in the production of such resources, as often an immediate response has been required.

The outcomes of the "Tragedy and Christian Congregations"[165] research project were reframed to apply to the experience of the pandemic. Materials for analysis and reflection were produced and publications sought to provide practical advice and guidance, and also raised wider questions about mission priorities in the crisis.

Every local church responds in its own context, in light of the nature of its buildings and their use and the capacities of the Minister, the eldership and the congregation. One size cannot fit all. Information and guidance on legislation needed to be continually updated through the phases of the pandemic. Decisions then had to be made locally in

---

165 https://tragedyandcongregations.org.uk/ [accessed 19th March 2021].

accordance with legislation and local circumstances, while ensuring that risks were minimised and mitigated and the environment was made as safe as possible. For example, detailed risk assessments were required for churches to reopen after the first lockdown but insurance liability lies with elders as local Trustees so there was no centralised system of approval of assessments or the giving of permission for churches to reopen.

It might be argued that there was and is potential for more joined-up thinking in the sharing of resources, in collaboration and the development of capacities, in mutual support, and in the birth of the new as well as for the maintenance of established patterns of Christian nurture, discipleship and faith.

TRAGEDIES AND CHRISTIAN CONGREGATIONS – THE PRACTICAL THEOLOGY OF TRAUMA

The research project was established under the leadership of Christopher Southgate in late 2016. The published volume[166] is a major component of the project's output, but the team continues to maintain a website, while also offering support to local clergy.

The initial intention was to explore the breadth of trauma experience in local Churches and congregations, but in fact focused on some specific trauma events that ensued (the Grenfell fire, the Manchester and London terrorist attacks) and the physiological effects of trauma, *applying*

---

166 Warner, M., Southgate, C., Grosch-Miller, C. A., Ison, H., 2020. Tragedies and Christian Congregations. Abingdon, Oxon: Routledge.

that knowledge to the experience of Christian congregations in the United Kingdom, with the goal of resourcing Ministers to lead their congregations through experiences of disaster and trauma response.[167] It has proved to be well placed to offer support and reflection through the Covid-19 pandemic and well timed to bring the results of the research to bear on that experience.

Part VI of the published volume is of particular importance, as it explores, from an informed and experienced perspective, *the implications of traumatic experiences for clergy care, self-care and training,*[168] including *the need for wisdom in the use of email and social media and the very physical needs of the body if it is to relax.*[169]

"READY FOR" AND "EMERGING INTO THE 'NEW NORMAL'"

The Synod Moderators of the United Reformed Church produced two documents to help churches prepare for the "new normal", the first in May 2020, "Ready for the new 'normal'",[170] a discussion paper, and the second, in June 2020, "Emerging into the new normal" replacing it and including aspects of policy. Although the Synod Moderators have no remit to agree policy, and it might be noted that the Moderators' meeting has also taken on a leadership role through the pandemic, this has made clear and swift responses

---

167 Warner, M. et al., eds, 2020 p.4.

168 Warner, M. et al., eds, 2020 p.257.

169 Ibid.

170 https://urc.org.uk/images/New-Normal-2020-v5.pdf   to   be superseded (see later) by "Emerging into the new 'normal'".

possible. The documents themselves were important as an early indication of the need and willingness to engage and respond at all levels. Information and instruction, advice and guidance were communicated quickly, avoiding the risk of being superseded and out of date. Social media and digital communication have also been essential.

In May 2020, the Moderators offered encouragement to the churches for the lifting of lockdown restrictions. However, it was recognised that there was uncertainty about when that would be and a cautious approach to the reopening of churches was recommended. Churches were encouraged to continue to pray for one another and for those charged with making difficult decisions.[171]

The papers, produced by the Moderators on the basis of expertise and careful research, were welcomed by other organisations. There was an urgent need and the distribution of the information and guidance was a priority. However, it is not yet known how many churches have responded to the more far-reaching questions the papers raised. They concluded with a bold statement, "We can have a new vision of what we want our churches to be like – what they might become rather than what they have been. There are so many things that we have been doing that were and are the right things, and we don't need to throw them away. But nothing should unthinkingly be carried forwards. The world has changed. It cannot go back to how it was, and in many, many ways, neither should it seek so to do."[172] If there is to be

---

171 Email received 7th May 2020.
172 Ibid.

significant change in mindset and the "new normal" is to be embraced, I suggest this is an important opportunity, but the statement needs to be accepted and owned by local churches, by Ministers of the Word and Sacraments and by the elders' meetings which share the leadership of those churches.

There are particular issues and challenges in keeping the fire burning for local churches already perceived to be running out of years. Some churches have already decided not to reopen; others might be encouraged to explore radical change. For some Ministers, elders and congregations, far-reaching challenges are not welcome. Others will enthusiastically and energetically embrace the "new normal" as what they have been working and praying for.

A further document complemented "Ready for the new 'normal'". Members of the Church Related Community Work and Mission and Discipleship teams, with Church Action on Poverty, produced "New reality, same Mission", for individuals and local churches to explore questions of community presence, engagement and social justice. The introduction stated: "We believe that Christians and churches are called to demonstrate God's love to our neighbours, and to collaborate towards building flourishing communities, so that people may live 'life in all abundance' (John 10:10). This is particularly important in this moment of crisis, reflection and rebuilding."[173]

Government legislation permitted places of worship

---

173 Downloadable at https://urc.org.uk/Church-information-guides/ 3485-new-reality-same-mission-a-stimulus-to-renewed-community-engagement-as-we-emerge-from-the-pandemic.html [accessed 24th May 2021].

177

to open for private prayer and, from July 4th, 2020, for public worship. Through the Moderators, United Reformed Churches were informed of these essential steps before reopening: (i) a written risk assessment to be sent to the Synod Office; (ii) Covid-secure measures (including social distancing and the washing or sanitising of hands); and (iii) informing the church insurers of the plans and that risk assessment and other measures are in place. Synod Moderators emphasised that the legislation was permissive and not prescriptive, and offered assistance and guidance.

The law continued to place significant constraints on worship. In particular, singing would be forbidden and the Moderators suggested this might influence any decision to reopen for worship. They also suggested that the summer might give time for preparation and further reduction in the infection rate. Furthermore, it was acknowledged that many churches would not reopen until September. The experience of separation had been difficult but it was essential to continue to take care of each other and not to act unwisely. Churches were urged to continue with a cautious approach. The duty of care was emphasised while it was acknowledged that steps needed to be planned towards reopening.

The papers circulated by the Moderators encouraged comprehensive review and resourced churches to reflect on their ministry and mission in light of the pandemic. I suggest that this might not have been the appropriate time for such review as churches and Ministers responded to more urgent demands. In due course there is likely to be more opportunity to reflect on the experience rather than respond in fast-changing circumstances. The documents may yet stand the test of time but in the crisis of the pandemic the task for the local church was to listen, assess priorities and respond to local needs according to its own capacity to do so. In the face of dislocation and disorientation, fragmentation and isolation, confusion and lack of clarity, the immediate need was to maintain, restore and rebuild relationships, in the fellowship of the church, with associated groups and in the wider community.

LEADING BEYOND THE BLIZZARD

Some ideas were developed by John Roberto and Praxislabs, a "creative engine for redemptive entrepreneurship, supporting founders, funders, and innovators motivated by their faith to love their neighbors and renew culture." [174] They describe three phases of crisis as blizzard, winter and mini-ice age.[175] The Church of England Birmingham Diocese produced resources based on these ideas.

In the first "blizzard" phase, resources are offered for immediate adaptation to crisis. This phase requires urgent and immediate response, practical steps to alleviate and survive the effects. Conditions are extraordinary and hostile and the need is for protection and shelter. Emotional and practical support are required, and relief is offered that is not sustainable for the longer term. This phase is short term and when it has passed we emerge into the same "normal". The fundamental task in the blizzard can be to wait.

---

174 https://www.praxislabs.org/ [accessed 23rd May 2021].

175 https://journal.praxislabs.org/leading-beyond-the-blizzard-why-every-organization-is-now-a-startup-b7f32fb278ff and https://www.lifelongfaith.com/uploads/5/1/6/4/5164069/.pdf [accessed 24th May 2021].

Examples of response might be the published resources and the workshops for the support of clergy provided by the "Tragedies and Christian Congregations" team, the pastoral care and practical support in congregations and more widely in neighbourhoods and communities, and the financial support through the government furlough scheme and, in at least one Synod of the United Reformed Church, assistance with the contributions to the Ministry and Mission Fund required from churches.[176]

In the second "winter" phase, the lockdown period and gradual emerging, some of the key aims are to establish sustainable spiritual and life rhythms which enable processing of challenges, and opportunities for deepening to occur. Protection is still needed as is adequate shelter. It can last for several months and is a season rather than an event so the response is different. Conditions can still be inhospitable and there are periodic incidents of severe weather which require further measures.

This was the context of much of the writing of this particular reflection.

In the third "ice age" phase, post lockdown, the key aims are to recognise how the landscape has changed, to discern what God has taught us in the lockdown, and to take the lessons and fruit of it into the future. This is to anticipate structural and cultural changes which will enable us to thrive in a time of changed resources. The consequences of an ice age are further reaching. A process of adaptation is

---

176 Ministry and Mission Fund – the means by which funds are contributed from the Churches to pay for Ministry.

necessary and change is large scale. Disruption is significant and potentially permanent.[177]

At the time of writing, in 2021, this remained a future aim. It is the phase into which local churches and communities, the wider Church and other institutions and organizations were hoping to move in the near future. The full impact and implications, however, remained unclear at that point with considerable anxiety and consistent calls for caution against the possibility of a third wave of the virus.

Roberto argues that there is no going back to a previous normal and we should respond and plan appropriately for the core mission of making disciples and nurturing faith for a lifetime. There is an opportunity for experiment to take us into a different future.[178]

LIVING AS DISCIPLES IN A TIME OF CRISIS

The initial response of the Lichfield Diocese of the Church of England was to produce a "Group Reflection Corona time" with questions for discussion and response and a commitment to listen and learn from the experience of others. Shortly afterwards an additional module in its "Living Discipleship" programme for training and equipping lay ministry was produced.

The module, entitled "Living as Disciples in a Time of

---

177 I am grateful to Guy Donegan-Cross, Director of Learning for Discipleship and Mission in the Birmingham Diocese for access to this material.

178 Roberto, J., n.d. Guide to transforming faith formation for a changed world. [Online] Available at: https://www.lifelongfaith.com/uploads/5/1/6/4/5164069/.pdf [accessed 11th March 2021].

Crisis" has four sessions: the first session encourages individual reflection on the experience of the virus and lockdown and includes a reflective exercise on separation; the second explores "Suffering and a God of Love". The third session is entitled "Worship in Extraordinary Time" and the final session, "Discerning God's Presence", explores the contributions of scripture, tradition and reason to Christian faith.[179]

This longer course is demanding but also allows depth and detail. It is perhaps indicative of expectations and capacities in the Diocese and may also reflect the nature of authority, energy and participation. This presents a challenge to the United Reformed Church in the knowledge, interpretation and application of biblical texts and the capacity to reflect theologically, but the Stepwise resources[180] currently being developed offer potential and encouragement.

THE VIRTUAL ENVIRONMENT

In 2019, before the Covid-19 pandemic, Mark Oakley wrote *We find ourselves spending life too tired to garden, too distracted to read, too busy to talk, too plagued by people and deadlines to organise our lives, to reflect on our futures, to appreciate our present. We simply go on, day after day after day. Where is what it means to be human in all of that? Where is God in all of that? How shall we get the most out of life if life itself is our greatest obstacle to it?* He goes on to suggest an answer: *You disengage to clarify and to connect at better depth.* [181]

179 I am grateful to Lindsey Hall, Discipleship, Vocations and Evangelism Strategy Enabler in the Lichfield Diocese for access to this material.
180 https://urc.org.uk/stepwise.html [accessed 24th May 2021].
181 Oakley, M. 2019 p.44.

This kind of experience may have been shared by many Christians and Churches before the pandemic. The pandemic brought additional pressures to bear and the range of the resources produced in response has been important. The "Tragedy and Congregations" team brought the reminder of the need for attention to self-care, the Synod Moderators provided essential advice and guidance on practical issues, and there are a variety of resources for reflection addressing the challenges and opportunities of mission engagement in these times. In addition, a variety of agencies, including charities such as Christian Aid and the Red Cross, have increasingly used webinars and online presentations to share information.

There has been no single "one size fits all" approach to Ministry in the pandemic. There are as many responses as there are Ministers and churches and the same Minister may respond differently in different churches in which they have pastoral charge. This arises from the varying capacity among elders and members, but the scoping of Ministry is also a contributing factor. There may be significant impact on the longer-term health and well-being of Ministers and others and it is open to debate how far this is inevitable. In the pandemic, there is an unavoidable loss of control and Ministers need to be resilient and flexible, responding to circumstances as they develop. Leaders might attempt to plan and define objectives and timescales, but all planning is contingent on factors beyond local control, and there may be rapid change in circumstances that will significantly influence the potential for action. All planning remains provisional, which for some increases potentially harmful stress but at the same time presents opportunities to take time, to tread lightly and to travel light, to take necessary steps while proceeding only one step at a time.

It is evident Ministers have played key roles in making decisions about reopening places of worship and determining the style, content and length of services as well as attending to practical matters such as risk assessments and social distancing. The picture is complex. A group of those in Synod appointments in the United Reformed Church with responsibility for development, explored the journey churches were making out of lockdown in September 2020 and recognised at least eight basic models. These were summarised (in no particular order) as:

A: A strong mixed economy
B: Telephone conferencing
C: Phased return to normal
D: Offline
E: Doing both (online and offline)
F: Ongoing adaptation
G: No rush to normal
H: National/local blend

The use of digital communication and social media has been and continues to be a key element, and there is discussion about the nature and validity of online church. Electronic media made a variety of resources available very quickly for those who were willing and able to access them. Communication in this way can be rapid and efficient and emails have on the whole facilitated and improved communication.

There are also disadvantages in electronic communication. The content of emails can be misinterpreted or misunderstood or an immediate response can be expected when that is either not possible or inappropriate. The convenience of emails and the ease of copying in sundry others can also result in a quantity of emails that becomes an obstacle rather than a benefit to good communication.

Social media (such as Facebook, WhatsApp, Instagram and Twitter) have provided the potential for mutual support, encouragement, information, advice and guidance. The United Reformed Church Ministers' Facebook group has demonstrated the potential of the closed group, restricted in membership, to share learning and practice and to be a forum for discussion and debate. It also has limitations; social media excludes as well as includes. Some may not have the capacity to communicate in this way while others choose not to do so. Further, social media are not "official" channels of communication and although it is likely that more participate as readers and followers than contributors a minority of Ministers are active participants. There is evidence of the presence and at least occasional if not regular participation of influential voices, including Synod Moderators and officers of General Assembly.

Online platforms (such as Zoom and YouTube) have played a substantial role from the outset of the pandemic. There was rapid progress from earlier experiments in the recording and live streaming of worship, which led to worship being shared in this way in many churches across the United Reformed Church. Churches and Ministers with the necessary expertise led worship "virtually"; nationally "Daily Devotion" extended to a weekly Sunday service.[182]

Such worship demonstrated considerable imagination and creativity, but there are more opportunities to make the most of the medium. Churches so far have tended to transfer their offline activity online, rather than adapting material for a new medium or seeking a new approach, style and content. Arranging online worship has however required considerable and arguably disproportionate investment of time and energy on the part of those responsible, the majority of whom have been Ministers of the Word and Sacraments. There have been limited opportunities to delegate or to group and share.

Practice varied in regard to the accessibility of recorded and streamed acts of worship. Some restricted attendance to those who had received the required electronic link, which ensured security and reduced risk, while others were made public. Some experienced more people "attending" than would have been the case in a physical setting, but this may indicate "passing traffic" rather than regular attendance.

There are distinctions between live streaming and recorded worship. Live streaming offers informality and warmth, immediacy, interaction and spontaneity while recorded worship enables a more polished and "professional" approach, at the risk of the loss of immediacy and omitting reference to events current at the time of broadcast. Both have increased the potential for participation and active engagement for the frail and vulnerable and particularly the housebound, and for those who have either moved

---

182 https://devotions.urc.org.uk/todays-daily-devotion/ [accessed 24th May 2021].

away permanently or are absent temporarily while working or on holiday. There is, however, a loss of engagement and participation for those unable or unwilling to develop access to the virtual environment and there will be further issues to be faced in the future, in the practicalities of providing continued access once physical gatherings are permitted. Discussions are in progress about the nature and potential and the next steps that need to be taken for "hybrid church" with online and in-person provision.

Some churches do not have the capacity, for a variety of reasons, to offer worship electronically and financial assistance is being made available for the purchase of hardware. Churches without online facilities and capacity have however maintained connectivity and contact in other ways, distributing printed worship materials or worship on CD or using telephone conferencing.[183] Theologically, the nature of presence and relationality in Christian faith and worship will need to be addressed. It is noted that on the Zoom platform it is possible to be present and heard but not seen.

With no congregational singing permitted, worship has relied on recorded material, allowing the use of material from a range of sources and in a variety of styles. A further implication for streamed and recorded worship has therefore been attention to copyright, and ensuring the appropriate licences are in place.

---

183 With thanks to Nick Stanyon, West Midlands Synod Evangelist. https://www.youtube.com/watch?v=R0JgqhXcT68 provides an overview of the range of approaches to worship in the pandemic across the United Reformed Churches in the Warwickshire and Coventry area of the West Midlands Synod [accessed 24th May 2021].

Superseding platforms such as Skype and Lifesize, the Zoom platform has become the "norm" for a range of meetings in the United Reformed Church, and particularly its Councils and Committees. It is being used for meetings of all kinds, formal and informal, one-to-one to large groups, teaching and decision-making. This practice, developed during the pandemic under lockdown conditions, is likely to continue in the future. It reduces or avoids the need for travel, allows for better use of time and gives attention to good practice in relation to climate change and protecting the environment. It has been acknowledged however that meetings online demand constant attention as well as focus on a screen, and can be particularly tiring, making adequate breaks essential for health and well-being as well as concentration. Virtual meetings may deal with business more quickly and efficiently than meeting face to face, with the added convenience and comfort of not leaving one's own home, but some opportunity for physical meeting from time to time is likely to be considered desirable and necessary.

In the United Reformed Church, the mind of Christ in decision-making is discerned in the meeting. It is therefore of particular importance to note that meeting online currently excludes as well as includes. There are issues relating to the reliability of the technology and full participation requires keyboard skills. Further exploration is needed on decision-making in this way, and particularly when controversial or complex issues need to be addressed. Robert Pope suggests that "Zoom" is not the ideal forum for seeking the mind of Christ as, in his experience, it seems to have increased the tendency to make decisions in executive bodies rather than in the council of the Church itself.[184]

Through the pandemic and repeated lockdowns attention has been given to matters of order and worship. There have been issues with regard to calling of Ministers into pastorates. Ordination and inductions have taken place virtually, but ordination has raised a specific issue with regard to the laying on of hands, which may be expected but is not required in the United Reformed Church. It is required practice in other denominations which share with the United Reformed Church in Local Ecumenical Partnerships. After some debate, the Ministries Committee have agreed practice for the United Reformed Church.

A further issue of theology and practice has been the conduct of Holy Communion online. In contrast to the understanding and practice of other denominations, online celebration is considered valid in the United Reformed Church, with participants providing their own bread and wine.

PASTORAL CARE

The pandemic has had serious economic and social consequences and the full implications for health and education are not yet clear. There is evidence of increasing incidence of mental ill health, domestic violence and abuse as well as growing concerns about large-scale redundancy and unemployment. Government schemes, of furlough and financial support, will come to an end, and there is a threat

---

184 Personal communication.

of far-reaching and long-lasting economic recession or even depression.

Pastoral care and mission engagement have continued in the pandemic and even in lockdown within the imposed constraints. Ministers and churches have continued to offer care for the vulnerable among their membership, in their local communities and in wider society. One issue in the reopening of churches however is the distinction between reopening for worship, reopening for groups supporting the vulnerable and marginalised, and reopening for groups who serve the community in other ways and are a vital source of income.

During the Covid-19 lockdowns Ministers and elders have responded by exercising pastoral care through regular telephone contact. In this way levels of connectivity have been maintained and even increased. Others have drawn attention to a loss of contact with those attending groups less formally attached to the local church and there have been significant challenges in end of life care and the conduct of funerals. Early in the lockdown, there were difficulties relating to the provision of personal protective equipment (PPE) for care homes. Some Ministers have conducted funerals frequently, while others have conducted very few. At the outset of the pandemic, Synod Training and Development Officers in the United Reformed Church collaborated in the production of liturgical resources for funerals but the most significant challenges have been in supporting grieving families who often had little or no contact with loved ones in their final days and weeks and no opportunity for a final goodbye. No physical meeting has been possible in preparation for funerals and the funeral itself has been conducted in a "Covid-safe" manner, which did not allow singing.

IMPLICATIONS FOR THE FUTURE

From March 2020, as the infection spread and the Government made its response, churches established a variety of practices with considerable imagination, creativity and energy. The impact on Ministers and the Ministry of the Word and Sacraments however has been considerable. It has been those ordained to Ministry of the Word and Sacraments who have borne the brunt of the changes that needed to be made, the measures that needed to be put in place, the learning that was necessary to enable the life of the local church to continue. Ministers have shared their experience of the increase in workload in preparing online worship and maintaining connectivity with those who were not able to access the technology. Some Ministers were better equipped and able to respond than others.

The impact will, in some ways, in some places, for some people, be temporary, while for others it will be permanent. Nevertheless, a "new normal" is taking shape for the short, medium and long term. At this particular point on the journey, we do not know what the future holds. Some will want to continue with the benefits that the lockdown has brought in the increased use of technology, continuing to meet online as possible and as appropriate. This will require investment in two ways – financial investment in the provision of the necessary hardware and software and the investment of time in training people, preferably more than one in each congregation, in the use of the equipment. This should be neither the task nor the responsibility of the Minister of the Word and Sacraments; there is a role for the wider Church in establishing and maintaining consistency and good practice.

Discussions have continued through the lockdowns across the United Reformed Church on the deployment of Ministers. Churches make decisions as they consider their future viability and some have already decided not to reopen. Some churches embrace the opportunities provided by digital communication and meeting in new ways, others are fearful and experience threat and the potential of being overwhelmed, and recognise that they are running out of years. Yet we continue to affirm the grace and the faithfulness of God. "*Nec tamen consumebatur.*" The fire – of faith, hope and love – continues to burn.

Ministers are not in competition with one another but respond within their own capacity, needs and resources. A primary concern must be with Ministers' self-care. As the pandemic continues, even with the roll-out of the vaccine, Ministers experience pressure and stress on their personal health, as well as their social and domestic circumstances, not to mention their role, identity and capacity as Ministers and leaders in the United Reformed Church.

Uncertainty continues; there is as yet no clarity for the "new normal". Churches and Ministers must continue to respond to their own context and circumstances and within their own capacity for action. Such factors determine and shape Ministry, rather than prevailing expectations of the style and content of worship, discipleship and mission.

Some churches will inevitably "run out of years" and take steps towards closure. There will be consequences for the deployment of Ministry, but the limitation of the number of Ministers available is already resulting in serious and far-reaching discussion which must lead to action. Under present proposals every local church will not receive the ordained Ministry they feel they need and a "mixed economy" is likely to develop by design or default. Some Ministry will continue on the existing and long-established model, meeting the expectations of churches, using the gifts, skills and experience of those exercising Ministry. Others will welcome and embrace a pioneer model. Some churches will respond to the opportunities the pandemic has brought to their attention with the finance and personnel to equip themselves, while others might be encouraged to take steps to reinvent themselves to serve their community.

Electronic media divide as well as connect yet offer vast potential for development and change. Attention will be needed to investment of time and energy as well as finance. The exercise of leadership will require communication, participation and collaboration. All who serve in formal roles in local churches – lay preachers, elders and Church Related Community Work Ministers as well as ordained Ministers of the Word and Sacraments – will need encouragement and support and, if necessary, challenge, to work and serve in this way. Partnership will be key – it is essential to acknowledge the validity of another's experience and practice as well as one's own, while being prepared to learn, develop and change.

Virtual and physical meeting are both vital in proclaiming the gospel and building the kingdom of God. Both are necessary to the church's task in ministry and mission. Churches need to be clear about their purpose and explore how that might best be achieved, how the gifts and resources at their disposal might be used to share good news.

The Covid-19 pandemic has brought discomfort and shock. This is not the world we expected or planned for, but the pandemic has also reminded the United Reformed Church of the diversity in Ministry already in practice. Any significant change across the Church will take time and we need to be prepared to commit to change while accepting difference and variety of practice as the norm. Training will be needed for diverse models of Ministry of the Word and Sacraments but in response to the needs expressed by local churches. Responsibility for change does not lie with the Minister but with the Church and institutionally begins not in the councils of the Church but at the grassroots, in local churches and communities.

In the August 2020 issue of the *Current Archaeology* magazine, author and regular contributor Chris Catling refers to the fear that church buildings closed for the pandemic will not reopen, and the rate of closure will increase. He suggests, *When a place of worship closes, you lose the focus of community life* and outlines all that is lost from a social and community as well as the historical and conservation perspective. He concludes *These buildings are the most significant heritage asset in our communities, the embodiment of architectural, historical, evidential, associative and community value.* Catling is aware of the church as a place for quiet prayer and contemplation but presents the case for maintaining church buildings for community use. He ends the article, *What is needed now, as the lockdown lifts by baby steps, is to invite everyone to get to know their local building and realise what a gem it is and how much it should be treasured.*[185]

Ultimately, however, the church is not buildings but people. The calling to Christian discipleship is a call to relationship, to engagement and connection, to form community. In community, worship is offered, disciples are formed and hope is embodied. Mark Oakley, reflecting on the tenth anniversary of the 9/11 terrorist attack on the Twin Towers in New York, wrote, *the invitation that lies in this remembrance is to see that our relationships matter more than anything else and that we should treasure them and each other with everything we have.* He continued, *God's gift to us is our being. Our gift to him is who we become. As a society it means translating the priority of love into the priorities of justice and equality. It means supporting the vulnerable, all those who live and work peaceably and those who support the common good.*[186]

Ministry of the Word and Sacraments plays a vital part. During the Covid-19 pandemic there has been widespread loss of relationship in churches and communities alongside a rise of community spirit, of mutual caring and concern in practical ways, but the restriction on meeting together and the requirements of social distancing have had a significant impact. Ministry in and through the churches, I suggest, can provide leadership in rebuilding and restoring relationships, bringing healing and support, incarnating the love of God made known in Christ and living out his will in service

---

185 *Current Archaeology* August 2020.
186 Oakley, M. 2019 p.165-166.

and discipleship. Ministry can be positive about the future, trusting in God and looking to the coming of the kingdom, recognising the opportunities for re-evaluation and change that even pandemic brings.

What might the future expression of the United Reformed Church look like? The common element may be that there are few common elements. The offering of worship may be mixed mode with pattern, style and content that is locally appropriate, arising from the shared life of the individuals who form church in a specific place, whether in physical or virtual space. Words, music, space, shape, forms and silence will be used in creative and imaginative ways to bring people into the presence of God and respond to God's love made known to us in Christ. Fellowship will be shared in different ways in different places, in virtual and physical meeting, in the sharing of stories and mutual support and encouragement, in co-operation and collaboration in discipleship, witness and service. There will be opportunities and challenges in reading the Bible together, discerning God's living Word for God's people today. There will be new possibilities for the life of prayer, for spiritual growth, for the building of faith. There will be joy.

The September 2020 email newsletter of CPAS, an Anglican evangelical mission agency, discusses leading through uncertainty. "The autumn term has arrived. September. The start of not only the new term, but for many of us in church life, the start of a new year. I have a hunch. We're not starting this term where we hoped we would be. Two months ago, we may have hoped lockdown was easing, normal worship services were resuming, and life was progressing into whatever the 'new normal' was to be. But we're not there, the defining reality is still uncertainty, and there may yet be a long way to go. Who knows how long and in what ways COVID [sic] is going to continue? Who knows when we will be able to sing together and share fellowship together (including coffee and an appropriate hug)? Who knows what 'normal' is going to be and when it might come?"[187]

The CPAS writer recognised that in the progress of the pandemic Ministers had responded energetically and creatively and also with anxiety and a sense of struggle. Ministers faced pressures and stress which they had never faced before and had not been faced by their forebears. This remains, the article suggested, uncharted territory and leaders can only respond with the wisdom available to them, seeking to discern the right time to open buildings, while being the target of others' anxieties, losses and frustrations, unable to engage in rational and straightforward planning, grateful for time off when free to take it yet unable to experience the refreshment and renewal of holiday.

The contributor went on to suggest that the leader's response should be to give up and so be released to embrace where we are and take up the reins once again, turning to God and those around us for help. This giving up takes these forms:

- Give up thinking you are the only one feeling this way, struggling this way. You are not alone. It is normal

---

187 CPAS Lead ON September 2020.

in a time of huge uncertainty to feel somewhat lost, frustrated, fed up.

- Give up thinking it is entirely up to you. God hasn't given up, and that is our single biggest source of encouragement. God is not surprised by anything that is happening. God is still at work, and wants to help us through.

- Give up trying to come up with a grand plan, and instead focus on some small wins, small things that can be done that build hope and help those we lead head in the right direction.[188]

In May 2021 the life of the Church continues to be sustained and nurtured by its Ministers of the Word and Sacraments. This Ministry in the living Church embodies discipleship, living the life of Jesus today, holding fast to values and principles of life and faith. Ministry points to God's faithfulness, wisdom and love. Ministry links past, present and future, and equips the Church to be the Church, the sign, instrument and foretaste of the kingdom of God in, through and beyond the Covid-19 pandemic. Ministry continues in confidence, holding fast to the theological principles that have brought us this far, while recognising the constant need for change, and for lifelong learning. There is always the risk of running out of years, but Ministry does not give up and continues to keep the fire of hope burning. As Paul writes to the Christians in Corinth: *So we do not lose heart. Even though our outer nature is wasting away, our inner nature is*

---

188 Ibid.

being renewed day by day. For this slight momentary affliction is preparing us for an eternal weight of glory beyond all measure, because we look not at what can be seen but at what cannot be seen; for what can be seen is temporary, but what cannot be seen is eternal (2 Corinthians 4:16-18, *NRSV*).

CONCLUSION

Life during the pandemic has been dominated by the experience of separation and isolation, by social distancing, the wearing of masks and by repeated lockdown with its limitations and restrictions on meeting and movement. Ministry in contrast is seen to be most effective and conveys the most meaning when it is fully interpersonal, representative, relational and incarnational, when the one exercising Ministry can be fully personal to another.

Yet Ministers have demonstrated through persistence and perseverance that there are other ways. Obstacles can be overcome, and fruitful Ministry can be exercised in and through struggle and suffering. This is not to downplay or devalue the experience, but to recognise that the pandemic and lockdown have provided opportunities as well as constraining activity.

Ministry of the Word and Sacraments, working together and developing patterns of collaboration and collegiality, must continue to provide leadership and vision for local churches, leading and enabling the Church to be the Church, the sign, instrument and foretaste of the kingdom of God. Gifts of creativity and imagination, alongside a depth of spirituality, help others inside and outside the Church to make the connections between faith and life, church and community, church and world.

Fruitful Ministry is energised in living and daily encounter and dependence on God and the scriptures, but will be subject to demands and expectations. Support is essential and Ministers are encouraged to engage with spiritual direction, mentoring or supervision to develop resilience and confidence to respond to challenges and opportunities.[189] Ministers should also engage systematically in theological reflection, developing awareness of their own and others' spiritual development and growth.

Ministers provide oversight for the core tasks of the church's life and witness, leading worship, providing pastoral care and offering leadership to the church for its role in the world, and need to be theologically educated and articulate, recognising the value of tradition while being unafraid of change.

Consistency might be established across the United Reformed Church with respect to lay leadership and eldership challenged and equipped to fulfil their calling and the responsibilities of the elders' meeting with respect to mission and wider ministry. Ministers need to be pastorally sensitive and aware. All exercise of Ministry is rooted in mutuality, but with clear accountability.

Ministers need to be prepared to take risks, to be flexible, to experiment and to learn from their own and others' experience, recognising their own vulnerability and limits and the opportunities presented in weakness as well as in strength. Through the experience of the pandemic, it has been recognised that "it is OK not to be OK". Ministers have

---

189 Professional pastoral supervision is mandatory for Ministers in the United Reformed Church from 2023.

been under pressure and unusual stress, and are encouraged to look after themselves and each other, to take appropriate time off. Ministers need to model good self-care, to resource themselves through rhythm and routine as far as is possible, regular rest and renewal.

Ministers must not be the sole resource in the local church for technological development and change. Technology may be key to change in many aspects of the Church's life, but as a means to an end and not an end in itself. The central challenge to the Church is not technological, financial, or social or in relation to its governance, but spiritual. It therefore requires a spiritual response. There may be a moment of opportunity and decision; in the use of available resources within and the limitations and constraints imposed from outside, the local church might be renewed in its faith and life, its ultimate trust in God, sharing good news, bearing witness to the faithfulness of God as saviour, provider, restorer, and protector. God continues to care; we find God not necessarily resolving the chaos and confusion of Covid-19 through which we live but, surely and certainly, in God's time, redeeming it.

Churches and the United Reformed Church may be running out of years but the fire still burns and we can dare to be reshaped into a "new normal". The clock may be ticking but *now faith, hope, and love abide, these three; and the greatest of these is love* (1 Corinthians 13:13, *NRSV*). There are arrangements to be made, decisions to be taken, programmes to be run, policies to be framed, but most importantly there are relationships to be nurtured for all human flourishing.

The Church needs to explore how change happens in today's world – from the centre or the edge, from the top or the bottom, from the local or the national or a haphazard yet organic combination of them all. Through pandemic and beyond, attention needs to be given to old and new practices and decisions made on what stays and what goes, who decides and how, holding true to the precepts, the values and the principles that have brought us this far and do not imprison us but free us for the future. Careful consultation and negotiation will be needed, locally, regionally, ecumenically and wider, ready to embrace flexibility on the one hand but avoiding the reinvention of too many wheels on the other.

Joy in worship and discipleship, mission and service might be lost in details of planning and execution, or simply making the technology work. We need to reap the fruits of experience of the kingdom present among us, recognising the future is not in our hands. We are called to participation in God's mission; in God's hands the future, as the past and the present, is safe.

This reflection, on Ministry in the pandemic in the United Reformed Church, began with a recollection of celebration, the excitement and anticipation of a wedding, without doubt one of the happiest days of my life. It ends in continued anticipation. These are times of preparation and looking forward, even in the face of uncertainty. The world waits and plans and prepares in the darkness of the pandemic. Yet the *light shines in the darkness, and the darkness did not overcome it* (John 1:5, *NRSV*) and, as it is said, the deepest darkness is just before the dawn. In spite of and through uncertainty, chaos and confusion, doubt, dislocation and disorientation, isolation and even desolation, there is always hope. There is always hope in the promise and fulfilment of new life, the promise of God to us, in Christ, of life in all its fullness: *The thief comes only to steal and kill and destroy. I came that they may have life, and have it abundantly* (John 10:10, *NRSV*).

QUESTIONS FOR DISCUSSION

- What has been the impact so far of the Covid-19 pandemic in your experience of worship, fellowship, discipleship and mission?
- What have you learnt from the experience?
- What do you see as the most significant and lasting changes in the Church and in society that will be direct consequences of the pandemic?

NINE

REFLECTION 7

ON ENDINGS

INTRODUCTION

I first discovered the poetry of Stevie Smith in my late teens or early twenties: the local amateur theatre group staged a production of *Stevie*, a stage play based on her life, later made into a film starring Glenda Jackson. I was particularly struck at the time with the sadness and pathos of "Not Waving but Drowning":

> "Nobody heard him, the dead man,
> But still he lay moaning:
> I was much further out than you thought
> And not waving but drowning.
> Poor chap, he always loved larking
> And now he's dead

It must have been too cold for him his heart gave way,
They said.
Oh, no no no, it was too cold always
(Still the dead one lay moaning)
I was much too far out all my life
And not waving but drowning."[190]

It is essential that we read the signs of the times and local communities well, hear the voices and see the waving of local churches, to discern where they are now and the appropriate response.

Malcolm Guite offers forty poems and reflections on the themes of loss, lament and hope in a book written *to give voice both to love and to lamentation, to find expression for grief without losing hope.*[191] Dylan Thomas, in his poem "Do Not Go Gentle Into That Good Night" suggests the response to death should be resistance and struggle, holding on to life. "Rage, rage against the dying of the light." His earlier poem, however, "And Death Shall Have No Dominion", offers a different and more explicitly religious prospective. The title line, taken from Romans 6:9, bookends each of three nine-line stanzas. The poem's energy and drive, rich and diverse images, and wordplay and apparent paradoxes, all convey the message that, in spite of the reality of the experiences of death, life goes on. [192]

190 Smith, S. 2015. Reproduced with permission of the publisher.

191 Guite, M. 2017. *Love, Remember* p.ix.

192 Thomas, D. 2016. *The Collected Poems of Dylan Thomas: The Centenary Edition.* London: Weidenfeld and Nicolson © The Dylan Thomas Trust.

Christian vocation, the life of faith, and the Ministry of the Word and Sacraments in particular, proclaims the gospel, the good news of Jesus Christ crucified and risen. It is apparent that church-going is decreasing and institutional organised religion is under threat, but the role of the Ministry of the Word and Sacraments remains, to inhabit the gospel that we proclaim and to enable others to share that inhabiting and not simply to visit this world or escape from it but engage meaningfully and purposefully with it. It is to live with the reality of death and yet proclaim good news, and to do so in Christian hope and love, maintaining a sense of awe and wonder in the face of the living God revealed to us in Christ. The Ministry of the Word and Sacraments keeps the fire burning, not defending the Church, maintaining it or seeking its survival but seeking its health and well-being as the sign, instrument and foretaste of the kingdom of God. This Ministry points the way to peace, love and justice, on the road to healing and hope, to fulness of life, to joy.

Stevie Smith concludes another of her poems, "Pad, Pad":

"Ah me, the power to feel exaggerated, angry and sad

The years have taken from me. Softly I go now, pad pad."[193]

In his discussion of the final lines of this poem, the stand-up comedian, television and radio host, author and podcaster Frank Skinner writes: *The whole poem, it seems now, has been an effort to conjure up a past emotion that isn't quite there any more. Or has it? The speaker doesn't, we're told, feel angry or sad like they used to. I especially love the idea of losing the 'power to feel exaggerated'. That is such a sharp image of what being in love is like, the complete loss of the middle register.*[194] He

---

193 Smith, S. 2015. Reproduced with permission of the publisher.

194 Skinner, F. 2020 *How to Enjoy Poetry (Little Ways to Live a Big Life)*

continues: *Our response, shot through with all our experiences, foibles, fears, attitudes, aspirations, completes a poem. The ending of 'Pad, Pad' has a lot to do with the reader. Is 'the power to feel exaggerated' a power or is it a weakness? Is losing that capacity for emotional intensity a loss or a liberation?*[195]

Skinner concludes, *That last couplet could be read as a tragic admission: the speaker's light has gone out, all passion subsided. These things were, it seems, not given up voluntarily, not put to one side. They were, the speaker explains, 'taken from me'. But, for me, that 'pad pad' – the voicing of it – changes everything. It is one last look back at the audience, a parting smile. This is Stevie Smith at her most Music Hall. The performer opens their heart to the audience but still leaves them laughing. There is also something cat-like about 'pad pad'. It gives the ending a tone of feline indifference, of Sphinx-like inscrutability, of triumph.*[196]

There might be an analogy here with Ministry of the Word and Sacraments. How are Ministers of the Word and Sacraments, called to give themselves to this demanding and yet rewarding vocation, to be energised and sustained? What keeps the passion alive and emotions engaged? How are endings addressed?

In her intriguing *Red Thread – on Mazes and Labyrinths*, Charlotte Higgins, classicist and chief culture writer of *The Guardian*, tracks the origins of the story of the labyrinth, and follows the idea through excavations and development across history, including religious settings such as the mediaeval cathedral in Chartres, while also tracing it in writers and

---

p.47. © Frank Skinner 2020. Reproduced with permission of the Licensor through PLSclear.

195 Ibid. pp.48-49.

196 Ibid. p.50.

artists. In so doing, and in reflecting on personal experience, the author explores what it is to be lost, to find one's way, and to travel the path of life.[197]

It is not unusual to struggle with endings which are often uncomfortable. According to Higgins, the great Classical poets, Homer and Virgil, share that struggle. *Epics often have problems with endings*, she writes.[198] Endings are associated with change and loss, remind us of our own vulnerability, mortality, even insignificance and bring a challenge to the meaning and purpose of life. Although closure and the opportunity to move on might be welcome in human experience, it is often difficult to recognise and define completeness and it is rarely possible to tie up all the loose ends.

The "red thread" of Higgins' title runs through the author's imagination, but, in the course of discussion of epic poetry in a section entitled *Out of the woods*, she writes: … *epic poems are also like life. We cannot remember our beginnings, nor, generally, do we have a feeling for how things are going to end. We experience life as the middle.*[199] For me, this statement encapsulates much of the story of any particular local church and of the United Reformed Church as a denomination. Some will remember local beginnings, and some the birth of the United Reformed Church in 1972. The end of such historical entities is unknown – we experience life in the middle.

It is also true of any individual Ministry of the Word and

197 Higgins, C. 2018.
198 Higgins, C. 2018 p.168.
199 Ibid. p.168.

Sacraments. We may fondly remember the experience of call, the act of ordination and a deepening sense of vocation, but we cannot know the end. Again, we experience life in the middle. Yet there is a thread that runs through it all, in spite of appearances to the contrary, twists and turns, paradox and contradiction. There is a sense of direction, a direction of travel. In the analogy of the labyrinth, however often the path leads away from the centre, apparently around in circles or back on itself, there is only one way, and the path leads inexorably and inevitability to the centre, where, one day, in God's good time, we will arrive.

For the moment, we may experience life in the middle, but there are endings.

THE UNITED CHURCH, HALESOWEN
APPROACHING CLOSURE

In human experience, there is a time for arriving and for beginnings, but a time too for leaving and for endings. Endings are of course inevitable. How do we end? How do we leave?

In October 2016, I concluded my Ministry at the Halesowen United Church with these words: "the last eleven years have been interesting times, times of remarkable change in so many areas of human life. As God's people seeking to discern his will and purpose you need not fear the future. It may be different, but we recognise that different is neither good nor bad – it is simply different. We point always to the faithfulness of God, his abundant provision for our needs and his continuing blessing. The God who has journeyed with us over these years continues to go with us."

I said, "There may be changes ahead and we may not welcome them, but we recognise that the power is not ours but belongs to God and God alone. We are human and sometimes we doubt and fear for the future, but to be a follower of Jesus is to be known and loved by God. God values and accepts us for who we are. God brings the church into being. God nurtures our life and sustains us. That is our beginning and that is where I end."

In August 2021, Steve Faber, Moderator of the West Midlands Synod of the United Reformed Church, posted this on the URC Ministers Facebook Group: "First day back after a fortnight's leave: in the inbox are emails about two churches deciding to close. I'm not sure I dare take any more holiday."[200] In the interchange that followed he offered the telling comment, echoed by others from their own experience even in larger churches, "A combination of pandemic and running out of local leadership – no one willing to take over from eighty/ninety-year-old elders. It is the local leadership that seems to be the biggest issue in both cases. Which makes me somewhat anxious that there are several more to come."[201]

In a subsequent post, Steve responded to a question from former Synod Moderator Elizabeth Welch, asking whether he could say which churches they were. He posted in response: "Welsh Frankton (only a question of when rather

---

200 https://www.facebook.com/groups/1521226424814180/posts/ 2967789473491194 Posted 16th August 2021 5.07 pm [accessed 3rd November 2021].

201 https://www.facebook.com/groups/1521226424814180/posts/ 2967789473491194 Posted 16th August 2021 5.45 pm [accessed 3rd November 2021].

than if as I'm sure you will know) and Halesowen which has undergone a very rapid decline sadly."[202]

My initial response was shock, then frustration and anger, perhaps particularly because the news had reached me through social media in this way, while I myself was on holiday, then sadness and regret. I had been party to some discussions and concerns expressed in Synod Committees but I was not prepared for this. My son Jonathan, visiting us on holiday, helped me to deal with that immediate response, and to "park" the reaction for the duration of the holiday and then to allow time to reflect, in the light of his own knowledge and experience of the United Reformed Church and Halesowen itself, where he had completed his A levels at the College of Further Education.

On 18th August I received an email from the church secretary, following up a correspondence around the sudden death of a previous church secretary a few weeks before. He wrote: "You may also have heard that we have decided to close the church, and I have been asked to see if you could be available on either 3rd or 10th October to take the last service."[203] On reflection, I recognised this is an enormous privilege, but one I could not pretend was an easy task.

Exploring the context of the decision to close, I had a conversation with Steve Faber, who had tried to reach me before the Facebook postings but been unable to do so, and then met with the church secretary and treasurer and another

202 https://www.facebook.com/groups/1521226424814180/ posts/2967789473491194 Posted 16th August 2021 7.02 pm [accessed 3rd November 2021].

203 Personal communication.

key figure in the life of the church, for whose support and assistance in difficult times I was and remain particularly grateful.

In the weeks leading up to the service, drafting the order and preparing the address, it was possible to begin to come to terms with the experience and the events, and so to offer content that was honest but also hopeful. I would be addressing the congregation as a Minister of the Word and Sacraments but in a significantly different role to that of the Minister in pastoral charge of the congregation. It was important and necessary to acknowledge the perceived lack of understanding, leadership and support from the denomination, and to express regret for what might have been and what might have been different. At the same time realism was essential, the acceptance of what had taken place, that life had moved on and there is no going back. Against that background it was also right and fitting to offer thanksgiving while accepting that even good things come to an end in God's good time.

THE CLOSING SERVICE – 3RD OCTOBER 2021

Introducing the closing service, I said:

"We gather this morning to say thank you and goodbye to this special place, where Christian worship, fellowship and service have been shared over so many years.

"We gather to mark this ending, with a mix of emotions; sadness, regret and a sense of loss and an underlying deep sense of gratitude. We give thanks for all that has been shared here, all that has been given, all that has been received from being part of the life of this place.

"There is much to celebrate today – stories from the past, years that have brought enrichment; God's continuing presence in love with us now; and God's promise of hope; God goes with us into the future with all its unknowns and uncertainties.

"We will listen and speak to God through prayer, through sharing stories, and through hymns of faith, chosen by yourselves. We will hear passages of scripture proclaiming the faith we hold, bearing witness to the love in which we are held, sustaining and inspiring us with hope for the future. We will reflect on all that has been accomplished in and through this place but the God who brings faith to birth in us travels with us on our continuing journeys. All our experience, all our life is rooted in Christian faith, so we will close today with the sacrament of holy communion, in which all are invited to share. The celebration of the Lord's Supper, sharing in the symbols of bread broken and wine poured, takes us back to the supper in the upper room that Jesus shared with his followers before his death and resurrection, and forward to the heavenly banquet prepared for us. Our sharing also sustains us now."

In the address, I said:

"We are not where we expected to be. But as I have reflected and planned over these weeks, I am coming to terms with the experience of vulnerability and fragility, with the uncomfortable reality of where so many churches now are. Time passes and life happens. God's grace and love are without limit but our resources are in some ways not limitless. Our call is to do what we can while we can, to use the gifts that we have been given while recognising they are

214

limited. There are beginnings and there are endings. There is a time for picking up, for taking on new responsibility and challenges but there is also a time for putting down. Fruitfulness depends on recognising times and seasons, planting and reaping. There are times when the right response is to recognise that a chapter of the story is ending, and the right thing to do is to draw a line under experience and to move on, without devaluing that experience, and give thanks for all that has been achieved through it.

"Today's mix of emotions is a natural part of the process of grieving. Endings can be uncomfortable and even painful. As you and I experience today's ending, there is so much that is being lost and so much that will be missed here; but we dare to affirm that even this, particularly this, is within the purposes, the goodness and the grace of God.

"We are called to faithfulness and fruitfulness in following Christ, and to bear fruit that will last. There is no doubt that the life of this place has borne fruit, in worship, fellowship, and service.

In worship: you have offered week by week, day by day, what is due to God, the God of power and love, grace and glory, God revealed in the weakness and frailty of human flesh, God made known to us in Christ, the image of the invisible God. Over so many years, faithful and fruitful worth-ship has been offered to God in and through Christ.

"In fellowship: you have shared faithfully and fruitfully in Christian community, in mutual care and concern, living and loving, laughing and crying together. Choirs and orchestras show us that different voices produce a greater sound and a sweeter song. Your lives have been enriched and enhanced through being shared, open to one another. That, I suspect, has not always been easy. Sometimes in life together there is disappointment, disagreement and even division, but you have followed in the way of Christ, the way to forgiveness, healing and wholeness, the way to unity in diversity, the way to harmony.

"In service: Your journey of faith has enabled you to go inwards, to know yourselves, to find God for yourself, to find truth that is truth for you. But you have gone outwards too, reaching out in response to needs beyond your own, serving in the name of Christ those outside the church, those your lives touch, the wider community and the wider world, the world that still desperately needs the good news of Jesus Christ, hope and healing, love and reconciliation.

"It is part of your story that you have not always been treated in the way or received the support you might have expected from the wider Church. But over many years, you have been nurtured and sustained together, in faith, hope and love. In being together, your lives have been enhanced and you have enriched one another as channels of the grace of God, and you have played your part in building a fairer, more just, more equal world. There has been abundant fruit. Now, however, you are on the brink of something new, something you do not know; the familiarity of this place will no longer be here for you. But the promise of God in Christ holds true: you will not be left alone; you live still supported by the everlasting arms, God's strength, God's wisdom, God's power made perfect in weakness, in wisdom, love and truth. You live still in God's continuing loving care and provision.

"*I appointed you to go and bear fruit, fruit that will last*

(John 15:16, *NRSV*). There are decisions still to be made, choices yet to make that will determine how far this is a comma, rather than a full stop, how far the end of a chapter, rather than the closing of the book, how far time for scene changes, rather than the final curtain. For now there are those mixed emotions. You are where you are – time has passed, life has happened. In life we know things do not always go the way we plan or expect. But as we mark this ending today there is still hope, there is always hope. The vision that brought this church into being might strengthen and inspire you for whatever lies ahead. God goes with you on the next stage of the journey and there is still, there is always, good news. It is God who brings the Church into being. It is God who nurtures our life and sustains us. And it is God who brings the life we know to an end, in the promise of a richer, fuller life to come. We are never beyond the reach of God's love, made known to us in Christ. That is our beginning and that is where, once again, I end."

ANALYSIS AND DISCUSSION

In my understanding, there were some clear factors that led to the decision of the church council and then the church meeting to close the United Church, Halesowen.

When the ecumenical partnership with the Methodist Church was ended in 2004, as a consequence of the Methodist Circuit taking the decision to expel the United Church (for reasons now largely lost in the mists of time but partly frustration over the provision of leadership) the church continued as a United Reformed Church with some members who had previously belonged to the Birmingham St

Halesowen United Church 2005
Photo Dorothy Carr (reproduced with permission)

Halesowen United Church Photo display 3rd
October 2021 "Easter breakfasts"
Original photos Annette Hadley Photo Jonathan Scott
(reproduced with permission)

Halesowen United Church 3rd October 2021
Photo Jonathan Scott (reproduced with permission)

Church that had closed to form the partnership. The church maintained the name "Halesowen United Church" and the structures that had been in place in the partnership. In particular, elected representatives formed a church council, some of whom were ordained elders of the United Reformed Church.

In the passing of time, no new elders were elected and ordained and at the time of closure there was a single serving elder. No one from among the church members was willing to take on the role and share responsibility, or, expressed in another way, no one recognised a call to this important ministry in the United Reformed Church. From the institution and particularly the perspective of Synod officers and Committees, this lack of elders was perceived as a significant weakness. It was however in my view largely a consequence of allowing the "hybrid" structure to continue and the confusion of identity that resulted.

The vacuum in leadership was also experienced in another way. The church had been expelled from the Methodist Circuit as offers to provide Ministry of the Word and Sacraments through a long vacancy after the departure of a United Reformed Church Minister around 2000 had been rejected. In the years that followed, from 2000 to closure, the United Church, Halesowen, received very limited Ministry of the Word and Sacraments, the twenty-five per cent scoping in which I served from 2005 to 2016.

The challenge facing the church at the point of closure was the filling of significant vacancies, taking responsibility for lettings, for the maintenance of the property and as safeguarding officer. As no one was willing to take on these responsibilities, and in the light of the lack of elders to give the leadership needed in the United Reformed Church, the church council considered and then reluctantly agreed to recommend to the church meeting that the church should close. With considerable reluctance and regret, the church meeting accepted the recommendation, but even at that point it is possible that there was a mismatch of expectation, that is at least hinted at in Steve's post following those quoted earlier. Referring to Halesowen he wrote: "one of those (churches) that felt right and ripe for growth, I had thought."[204] The church was expecting more support from the Synod than the Synod was able to offer, arising from the shortage of Ministers of the Word and Sacraments; the Moderator, on the other hand, had been prepared to offer Ministry of the Word and Sacraments shared with another church, but perceived the Halesowen Church as being more fragile and vulnerable than he thought and believed a Minister would be faced with unrealistic expectations and demands.

I suggest the underlying loss of confidence in the church may be of greater significance in the bigger picture and the longer term than either the lack of leadership, the mismatch of expectations, or the issues around structures and identity. The loss of confidence in themselves, in the gospel and in the structures contributed to a lack of response in discerning vision and purpose and the opportunity to explore the mission of the Church going forward beyond the closure of the local church.

---

204 https://www.facebook.com/groups/1521226424814180/posts/ 2967789473491194 Posted 16th August 2021 8.56pm [accessed 3/11/21].

Further, in the absence of a strategic approach to ministry and mission, there was no opportunity for other churches to learn from the experience, for the church members to consider either individually or together possible options and scenarios for their own discipleship, worship and witness in other places, or to investigate possible new beginnings and other forms of expression of church. There was no consultation with the members that I am aware of to consider what might follow for them. The closing service was arranged so rapidly and at such short notice that at its close worshippers were left bereft with no point of contact with each other or with the church.

There are other issues around the closing of churches and enabling dying well and a good death on the one hand and attention to the potential for resurrection and new life on the other. There is an apparent lack of guidance and information for United Reformed churches and Ministers of the Word and Sacraments. Material from the Church of England[205] and the Baptist Union[206] applies to contexts so different from the United Reformed Church, particularly in relation to structures and decision-making processes, that very little is transferable. I argue that there is a specific need in the United Reformed Church for training and resources which requires an urgent response. This need is accentuated by two other significant factors – the Covid-19 epidemic and

205 https://www.churchofengland.org/sites/default/files/2020-02/Struggling_closed_and_closing_churches_report.pdf [accessed 3rd November 2021].

206 https://baptisttimes.co.uk/Articles/495753/The_time_has.aspx [accessed 3rd November 2021].

the consequent constraints and lockdowns, and the current emphasis and action with regard to the deployment of Ministers of the Word and Sacraments. Both have deepened the experience of vulnerability and precariousness and affected not only the worship and witness of local churches in practical ways but also the morale of Ministers and members in ways that may yet be found to be lasting.

There are questions to be addressed around the practicalities, mission engagement, legalities and pastoral issues of closing well. They concern church buildings, what God is doing in a place and in the lives of a congregation of God's people, legal requirements and obligations, and dealing with the experience of bereavement and loss and the impact of choices and decisions. Information and guidance as well as appropriate support are needed for all the stakeholders – Ministers of the Word and Sacraments, elders and churches, members, adherents, and community groups – who are on this particular journey. The approach must be strategic and proactive rather than reactive, piecemeal, and ad hoc and also address the issues positively, creatively and imaginatively, so that ways to healing and hope and through death to resurrection might be found and offered at a level at which those impacted might engage.

QUESTIONS FOR DISCUSSION

- What are the characteristics of a good ending, in literature and in life? What part do actions, feelings, implications and consequences play?

- Why does the human experience of endings often bring challenge, discomfort and regret? How might the church face its own endings, and equip and empower others, with realism and hope?

- Is a strategy for closing churches defeatist by definition? Who might best take responsibility for such a strategy? Who makes the decisions, and on what grounds, according to what criteria, and over what timescale?

- What is the likely ongoing and longer-term impact of the Covid-19 pandemic? Are there likely to be new opportunities and potential for local churches and their leadership to respond to human social and spiritual need?

- How might a "hospice ministry" for dying local churches be developed and supported? Is it a realistic possibility? Is such "hospice ministry" a distinct, specialised and separate role, or part of the role and responsibility of all Ministers of the Word and Sacraments? In either case, what are the particular training needs of churches, elders and Ministers?

TEN

FINAL CONCLUSIONS

LOOKING BEYOND THE COVID-19 PANDEMIC
AND INTO THE NEW NORMAL

Rowan Williams writes: *The past is never over, but it is not everything. A fierce clinging to what we have inherited from the past is never enough. We have to look at the new landscape and see freshly in this new setting what we remember. In the Church's life, it's the tightrope we tread between the amnesia that is so consumed by contemporary pressure and fashion that it never bothers to find out what the community's memory or tradition is saying, and the equally damaging traditionalism which idealises the entity we think we once were. Both of these refuse the really creative challenge of integrating "past selves" in a fuller understanding of the present.*[207]

T. S. Eliot's "Four Quartets" reflect on time, perspective, humanity and salvation. In the fourth, "Little Gidding", the

---

207 Williams, R. 2020 p.89.

poet uses the image of pentecostal fire to emphasise the need for purification. Humanity's flawed understanding has led to conflict; the narrator meets a ghost who combines poets and literary figures and lessons from the past to offer a way forward that is optimistic, focusing on the unity of past, present, and future, claiming that understanding this unity is necessary for salvation.

Eliot wrote:

"What we call the beginning is often the end
And to make an end is to make a beginning."
The poem concludes:
"We shall not cease from exploration
And the end of all our exploring
Will be to arrive where we started
And know the place for the first time.
Through the unknown, unremembered gate
When the last of earth left to discover
Is that which was the beginning;
At the source of the longest river
The voice of the hidden waterfall
And the children in the apple-tree
Not known, because not looked for
But heard, half-heard, in the stillness
Between two waves of the sea.
Quick now, here, now, always
A condition of complete simplicity
(Costing not less than everything)
And all shall be well and
All manner of thing shall be well

When the tongues of flame are in-folded
Into the crowned knot of fire
And the fire and the rose are one."[208]

In March 2021 a Synod Moderator presented evidence of significant decline in the membership of the Churches both before and during the pandemic. He wrote, "When I look at those (churches) that have made their (annual) return, I count 13 out of 108 that have lost **MORE THAN A THIRD** of their members in the last 12 months… When I look at those that have lost between 10% and 33%, there are 32 out of 108. Compare that with those reporting a growth (typically in single figures of members, most often by a single person, and single figures percentage), there are only 15 out of 108. Although we're still waiting for those overdue returns which should ease the position a little, we lost about 10% of members during 2019 and another 10% in 2020. We are in a deeply serious position."[209]

Also in March 2021, a paper was brought to Mission Council setting out a number of challenges: Covid-19, deployment and Ministry and Mission, the pension fund deficit, the risk our structures pose and who we are called to be. It was resolved to "appoint a small group to oversee a review of the structures, resources and work of the United Reformed Church to enable us to respond faithfully to the challenges set out in the paper". The paper concluded: "It is clearly time to ask ourselves some difficult questions about what we are called to leave behind, put

---

208 Eliot, T. S. 2002. Reproduced with permission of the publisher.

209 Steve Faber email to members of the Synod Missional Discipleship Development Committee 8th March 2021 – his capitals and bold type.

down, allow to go the way of the cross, to fit ourselves to be faithful in this moment. This will also release new resource and energy for new work in the future and we need to discern with wisdom where the seeds of resurrection are planted. We need to catch a vision of the possible, live into resurrection hope, and face with wisdom the tough challenges of the present."[210]

It is apparent that we have been here before, time and again. I suggest that what is needed now is not institutional change, attention to management or governance or structures, but a call to renewed faith and trust in God as the source of all life, and to the fundamentals of prayer and worship. The life of the local church is sustained and nurtured in worship. The Word and Sacraments build up discipleship. Such a renewal of faith and trust in God might lead to the renewal from the roots that is sought and in due course to more vocations to the Ministry of the Word and Sacraments, but, even if it does not, we hold true to the call to faithfulness.

The Ministry of the Word and Sacraments is vital to the life and health of the Church, providing consistency and theological integrity while recognising individual gifts and vocation. Ministers then should be centrally trained to be theologians and teachers rather than primarily enablers of mission. Mission is the inevitable consequence of life in the Spirit, as worship and prayer go beyond weekly liturgical Sunday activity, and sustain spiritual life day by day. It is

---

210 See United Reformed Church, 2021 *Future of the Church*. [Online] Available at https://urc.org.uk/images/MissionCouncil/March-2021/A1_Future_of_the_URC.pdf [accessed 15th July 2022] and United Reformed Church, 2021 *Church Life Review*. [Online] Avaliable at https://urc.org.uk/wp-content/uploads/1638/27/Paper_N2_-_Church_Life_Review.pdf. [accessed 15th July 2022].

not the God of the Church who needs a mission, but the missionary God who calls and equips a Church.

In the story of the United Reformed Church, the understanding of the place and purpose of the Ministry of the Word and Sacraments has not always been clear or consistent. Decisions have frequently been made on an ad hoc basis while at the same time proposals to change patterns have been repeatedly rejected. It has been suggested to me, by a former Moderator of General Assembly, that reports to Assembly have sometimes failed to focus on the central vision of the Church and the particular nature of the Ministry of the Word and Sacraments, acknowledging that all Ministry is in some sense missional but Ministers have given too much time and emphasis to their own involvement in mission and evangelism rather than teaching, training and equipping the whole people of God.[211]

Flexibility, imagination and creativity will be essential gifts for leadership; the precise form and shape of any particular Ministry will depend on context and the gifts available. The Mission Council paper might provide an opportunity for exploration but the key response will be from the local churches which are not static but dynamic and gifts can be discovered, discerned, and developed.

As we live through this time of crisis, alongside the loss of confidence in the gospel to change lives, there is the possibility of something new. John Proctor, writing in the Spring 2021 *In GEAR* newsletter of the Group for Evangelism and Renewal in the United Reformed Church says: … *the events of the last year or so, and the long-term damage these will do, have hurt*

---

211 Elizabeth Welch Personal communication.

many lives and homes. Much of the strain will last. As Church we may have two roles. One is to speak, to act, to help and to care, where we see hardship and injustice. The other is to be a stable, secure, and peaceful people, an anchor among our neighbours, and to live with integrity, calm and courage when the winds of change are swirling. All of this calls us to a deeper relationship with God. Proctor refers to the letter of James as a possible word for this moment, with *practices, values and hopes to shape us for the responsibilities ahead.*[212]

Ministers model and offer to the Church what the Church offers to the world. They need support – financial, spiritual, psychological and social – as they respond to God's call. Ministers also equip and train elders for their responsibilities in spiritual leadership. We need to be clear both about the change that is needed and where change might come from. A decade or so ago, John Bradbury (now General Secretary) presented some "reasonably random ideas to get us thinking" to a United Reformed Church conference. His ideas were these: re-engage with scripture, invest in worship, close churches, encourage theology, sort polity, ensure unity, build radical community, attend to oversight, renew understanding of vocation, and no fear.[213] He made no direct reference to mission strategy.

We need now to make the vital distinction between the urgent and the important. It might be perceived that the life and mission of a specific local church has come to an end or is in some sense no longer viable. I suggest there would

---

212 In GEAR Spring 2021.

213 The United Reformed Church 2012 Conference papers.

be greater encouragement, more hope, more joy and more likelihood of new vocations to Ministry of the Word and Sacraments, if we seek to sustain the life of the local church through a renewal of faith and trust. Action is needed now to discern and respond to local need rather than initiate increased centralisation with more authority, power or control entrusted to Assembly or Synod. The voices from local churches should be clearly heard and the response must be relevant and informed by the local context. Creative approaches might offer a way forward, but only if the local church is willing to support them.

Local churches with a traditional pattern of life and Ministry faithfully provide the majority of the personnel and resources supporting and enabling the Church. Educating the churches – and being a learning Church – must include reflection on their current circumstances and harsh realities particularly economically but continuing to trust in the promises and the grace of God. Then the churches might be led by the Spirit of God to be adventurous and take risks in supporting new forms of church life. The good news of Jesus Christ will be passed on in vibrancy and hope: instead of closing churches, gifts and resources might be released for them to reshape themselves to engage with the challenges and opportunities of their specific context.

I conclude that there are three areas that require urgent attention and action at all levels in the life of the United Reformed Church.

First, *leadership*; it is Ministry of the Word and Sacraments that must provide the foundation and inspiration for the church's life and witness, that encourages and nurtures faith, witness and discipleship. Only if such leadership is cherished and valued will it have the resilience to continue to proclaim the good news of the gospel through challenging and changing times.

Secondly, *relationship*; teamwork among Ministers and in elders' meetings including the Minister, consultation and collaboration both underpinned by gospel and kingdom values and for the sake of the gospel are vital.

Thirdly, *learning*; followers of Jesus are disciples. All must commit themselves to lifelong learning through mutual vulnerability and reflective practice. We cannot find all we need for faith and discipleship from within but are nurtured by prayerful and communal study of the scriptures and by the wisdom of the tradition.

If there is to be change, which I commend and urge, it might be co-ordinated through the wider Councils but must come from the edge either as well as or instead of from the centre. It must come from the places and above all the people in whom worship and mission, discipleship and witness are lived out, and through whom the gospel is preached in response to local needs and issues, opportunities and concerns.

On the journey of faith and in the story of the Church conclusions are never final. Urgent action may be necessary but measures we take are always provisional. There is always hope: the prospect and the fears of running out of years may be real for the denomination as for local churches. Against that prospect and with those fears we persevere, holding still to the Presbyterian motto "*nec tamen consumebatur*" – the fire still burns. As Rowan Williams writes: *He (Christ) is contemporary with me now; and when I remember with honesty and hope, I discover that he is contemporary with what I remember, faithfully at work in my past as in my present. And as I struggle and pray to bring together the fragments of an identity that is always being shaken around and remodelled, I get some glimpse of the promised end in which Christ simply embraces the whole of me, all I have been, and makes it one with itself and with him.*[214]

We reach a full stop. Running out of years? Certainly not! Decline, dying, and death are inevitable but there is new life from the dead, and the power of resurrection. *I want to know Christ and the power of his resurrection and the sharing of his sufferings by becoming like him in his death, if somehow I may attain the resurrection from the dead. Not that I have already obtained this or have already reached the goal; but I press on to make it my own, because Christ Jesus has made me his own.* (Philippians 3:10-12, *NRSV*). *So if anyone is in Christ, there is a new creation: everything old has passed away; see, everything has become new!* (2 Corinthians 5:17, *NRSV*)

For me, for these reflections, with retirement, whatever that may mean, on the horizon, it is time to make an ending.

"Ah me, the power to feel exaggerated, angry and sad

The years have taken from me. Softly I go now, pad pad."[215]

Neil Thorogood's *Westminster DNA* featured in the introduction to these reflections on the theology and practice of Ministry of the Word and Sacraments in the United Reformed Church. As I draw them to a conclusion, I offer another piece of art from a very different time and place.

---

214 Williams, R. 2020 p.89.
215 Smith, S. 2015. Reproduced with permission of the publisher.

Landscape with Moses and Burning Bush
Domenico Zampieri (Domenichino)
© The Metropolitan Museum of Art

In Advent 2019, the Transpositions website offered a series on "The Art of Advent: A Painting a Day" by Jane Williams.[216] Letizia Morley reflects on one of the Great Antiphons, *O*

216 https://www.transpositions.co.uk/the-art-of-advent-o-adonai/ [accessed 7th January 2022].

Adonai (Lord), and Domenichino's *Landscape with Moses and the Burning Bush* (1610–1616).[217] The painting is typical of the Italian Baroque style. Observation of nature is transposed to an idyllic, timeless realm.

Morley points out, "The backdrop looks like seventeenth-century Italy, which creates a jarring juxtaposition of the landscape to the biblical desert setting. The area around Moses seems to be desolate and scorched, but if you look beyond it you will see a lush paradise. Given Domenichino's roots in the Bolognese school of painting, it is likely this idealised scene is modeled loosely on a lake in northern Italy."

She continues, quoting Jane Williams, "*God draws Moses into dialogue that allows Moses to feel, even in the face of this overwhelming display of power, that he is still valued, his co-operation requested, not coerced. God is not enslaving Moses in order to free others. Freedom is God's goal and that means Moses' freedom, as well as that of the children of Israel.*"[218]

"God's call to Moses," Morley continues, "is a call to freedom in Moses's place and time. And yet it is also a timeless call to us across the ages. Coming back to the odd contrast of the Italian landscape to Moses's desert scene, I agree with Williams's view on this timeless relationship: *This happens to be Moses' encounter with the divine power, but it is happening in Domenichino's time and country. This happens to be God's call to Moses to fulfil his particular vocation, but,*

---

217 https://www.metmuseum.org/art/collection/search/436205 [accessed 7th January 2022].

218 Williams, J. 2018. *The Art of Advent: A Painting a Day.* London: SPCK. p.80.

by implication, the burning bush awaits any of us: we might come upon our encounter with God and God's call on our lives anywhere. Domenichino is urging us to attend, so that we will notice our burning bush and leave our accustomed path to investigate and so find out who we are."[219]

Morley then goes on to suggest that the scale of the painting indicates that the landscape is more important than Moses and deduces the creator is greater than an individual, who plays a small part in the whole story. Therefore, "This whole painting is a 'fill-in-the-blank' where we can visualise our own place in God's story and where we can imagine our own surroundings instead of an Italian lake."

I conclude: each of us has a part to the play in the unfolding story of God. Ministry of the Word and Sacraments has its own significance and contribution to the building of the Church and the coming of God's kingdom but as part of a much fuller picture. Moses is not at the centre of Domenichino's image but that is not to deny the vital part Moses plays in the story of God, in leading God's people out of slavery in Egypt and to the edge of the Promised Land. In our own time and place, there are those called to particular roles and responsibilities in the United Reformed Church, and endowed with particular gifts and receiving the calling to eldership, to the Ministry of Church Related Community Work and to the Ministry of the Word and Sacraments. Elders and Ministers of the Word and Sacraments together are entrusted with the responsibilities of providing leadership to the local church, while Church

---

219 Williams, J. op. cit. p.81.

Related Community Work Ministers are commissioned to serve alongside the local church providing the impetus for the work of the local church in the community in the places where they are appointed to serve. Ministers of the Word and Sacraments also provide leadership as Synod Moderators and in the wider Councils of the Church. In every case however there is an emphasis on shared leadership and the significance of relationship. Some are called to particular roles and responsibilities and not everyone can or should do everything but calling is to all. The priesthood of all believers is embodied as each individual lives out their own vocation.

So, I maintain, the fire still burns, as each and every individual in their own time and place discovers, responds to and fulfils their own vocation, God's call and claim on their lives. Some then in the United Reformed Church will offer themselves to serve as elders, others as Church Related Community Work Ministers and yet others as Ministers of the Word and Sacraments, for the building of the Church as the sign, instrument and foretaste of the coming of the kingdom of God in peace, love and justice.

I close with two hymns, from different traditions and very different times, prayers for this time and for the future. Firstly this invocation of the Holy Spirit, written by Charles Wesley (1707–88):

"O thou who camest from above
the pure celestial fire to impart,
kindle a flame of sacred love
on the mean altar of my heart!

236

There let it for thy glory burn
with inextinguishable blaze,
and trembling to its source return
in humble prayer and fervent praise.

Jesus, confirm my heart's desire
to work, and speak, and think for thee;
still let me guard the holy fire,
and still stir up the gift in me.

Ready for all thy perfect will,
my acts of faith and love repeat;
till death thy endless mercies seal,
and make the sacrifice complete."

Finally, this prayer for the continuing journey of faith, written by Caryl Micklem (1925–2003):

"Give to me, Lord, a thankful heart
And a discerning mind;
Give, as I play the Christian's part,
The strength to finish what I start
And act on what I find.

When, in the rush of days, my will
Is habit bound and slow,
Help me to keep in vision, still,
What love and power and peace can fill
A life that trusts in you.

By your divine and urgent claim,
And by your human face,
Kindle our sinking hearts to flame,
And as you teach the world your name
Let it become your place.

Jesus, with all your church I long
To see your kingdom come:
Show me your way of righting wrong
And turning sorrow into song
Until you bring me home."[220]

220 © Alison Micklem Reproduced with permission.

BIBLIOGRAPHY

BOOKS AND PRINTED DOCUMENTS

The Baptist Union of Great Britain and Ireland 1984. *Half the Denomination*. London: The Baptist Union of Great Britain and Ireland.

Barnes, M. C., 2009. *The Pastor as Minor Prophet*. Grand Rapids: Wm. B. Eerdmans Pub. Co..

Beeley, C. A., 2012. *Leading God's People; Wisdom from the Early Church for Today*. Grand Rapids: Wm. B. Eerdmans.

Brookner, Anna and Dunlop, Andrew, 2019. *Mixed Economy Mission MEv 126*. Cambridge: Grove.

Brueggemann, W., 1989. *Finally Comes the Poet; Daring Speech for Proclamation*. Minneapolis: Fortress Press.

Brueggemann, W., 2014. *Sabbath as Resistance*. Louisville, Kentucky: Westminster John Knox Press.

Brueggemann, W., 2017. *Sabbath as Resistance, New Edition with Study Guide: Saying No to the Culture of Now*. Louisville, Kentucky: Westminster John Knox Press.

Calvin, J., 1960. *Institutes of the Christian Religion*. 2 Vols. Tr. Ford Lewis Battles. Ed. J. T. McNeill. London: SCM.

Campbell, A. V., 1981. *Rediscovering Pastoral Care*. London: Darton, Longman and Todd.

Cornick, D., 1998. *Under God's Good Hand.* London: United Reformed Church.

Cornick, D., 2008. *Letting God be God: The Reformed Tradition.* New York: Orbis Books.

Davie, G., 1994. *Religion in Britain Since 1945; Believing Without Belonging – Making Contemporary Britain.* New Jersey: John Wiley and Sons Ltd.

Dewar, F., 2000. *Called or Collared.* 2nd ed. London: SPCK.

Donovan, Vincent J., 1982. *Christianity Rediscovered.* New ed. London: SCM Press.

Dudley, C., 1978. *Making the Small Church Effective.* Nashville: Abingdon Press.

Dulles, A., 1978. *Models of the Church.* London: Gill and MacMillan Ltd.

Dunlop, A., 2018. *Out of Nothing.* London: SCM Press.

Eliot, T. S., 2002. *Collected Poems 1909-1962.* London: Faber and Faber Ltd.

Fiddes, P., 2000. *Participating in God: A Pastoral Doctrine of the Trinity.* London: Darton, Longman, & Todd.

Fiddes, P., 2001. *Faith in the Centre: Christianity and Culture.* Oxford: Regent's Park College.

Gay, D., 2017. *Reforming the Kirk.* Norwich: St Andrew Press.

Greenleaf, Robert K., 2002. *Servant Leadership (25th Anniversary edition).* Mahwah, New Jersey, USA: Paulist Press.

Greenleaf, Robert K., 2003. *The Servant-Leader Within.* Mahwah, New Jersey, USA: Paulist Press.

Grundy, M., 2015. *Multi-congregational Ministry.* Norwich: Canterbury Press.

Guite, M., 2014. *The Word in the Wilderness.* Norwich: Canterbury Press.

Guite, M., 2017. *Waiting on the Word.* Norwich: Canterbury Press.

Guite, M., 2017. *Love, Remember.* Norwich: Canterbury Press.

Heifetz, R., 2009. *The Practice of Adaptive Leadership.* Brighton, Massachusetts, USA: Harvard Business Review Press.

Heifetz, R. and Linsky, M., 2017. *Leadership on the Line.* Brighton, Massachusetts, USA: Harvard Business Review Press.

Heifetz, R., 2000. *Leadership Without Easy Answers.* Cambridge, Massachusetts, USA: Belknap Press, Harvard University Press.

Higgins, C., 2018. *Red Thread – On Mazes and Labyrinths.* London: Penguin Random House.

Holland, T., 2020. *Revolutionary.* London: SPCK Publishing.

Inge, J., 2003. *A Christian Theology of Place.* Aldershot, Hampshire: Ashgate.

Kaye, E., Lees, J. and Thorpe, K. 2004. *Daughters of Dissent.* London: United Reformed Church.

Mann, P., and Wong, D., 2020. *Worship in Cyber Church.* Compass Publishing.

Marvin, E., 1995. *Shaping up Reforming Reformed Worship.* London: United Reformed Church.

McCarthy, M., Mynott, J. and Marren, P., 2020. *The Consolation of Nature: Spring in the Time of Coronavirus.* London: Hodder Studio.

Morley, J., 2016. *Our Last Awakening: Poems for Living in the Face of Death.* London: SPCK Publishing.

Moynagh, M., 2012. *Church for Every Context: An Introduction to Theology and Practice.* London: SCM.

Moynagh, M., 2014. *Church in Life: Innovation, Mission and Ecclesiology.* Oxford: Monarch Books.

Moynagh, M., 2017. *Church in Life: Innovation, Mission and Ecclesiology.* London: SCM.

Moynagh, M. and Milne, A., 2016. *The DNA of Pioneer Ministry.* London: SCM.

Newbigin, L., 1977. *The Good Shepherd.* Leighton Buzzard: The Faith Press.

Newbigin, L., 1978. *The Open Secret*. London: SPCK.

Newbigin, L., 1989. *The Gospel in a Pluralist Society*. Grand Rapids: Eerdmans.

Newbigin, L., 1995. *The Open Secret*. London: SPCK.

Oakley, M., 2019. *By Way of the Heart*. Norwich: Canterbury Press.

Oakley, M., 2019. *My Sour-Sweet Days: George Herbert and the Journey of the Soul*. London: SPCK Publishing.

Paton, D. (ed.), 1965. *New Forms of Ministry*. Edinburgh: Edinburgh House Press.

Peel, D., 2003. *Ministry for Mission*. Manchester: Northern College.

Peel, D., 2006. *Encountering Church*. London: United Reformed Church.

Peel, D., 2007. *Reforming Theology*. London: United Reformed Church.

Peel, D., 2012. *The Story of the Moderators*. London: United Reformed Church.

Percy, M. with others, 2014. *The Bright Field*. Canterbury Press: Norwich.

Pickard, S., 2009. *Theological Foundations for Collaborative Ministry*. Aldershot, Hampshire: Ashgate.

Pratico, G. D., and Van Pelt, M. V., 2014. *Basics of Biblical Hebrew Grammar*. Grand Rapids: Zondervan.

Rohr, R., 2016. *The Divine Dance: The Trinity and Your Transformation*. London: SPCK.

Rohr, R., 2018. *Just This: Prompts and Practices for Contemplation*. London: SPCK.

Rohr, R., 2019. *The Universal Christ*. London: SPCK.

Ross, C. and Baker, J., 2014. *The Pioneer Gift: Explorations in Mission*. Norwich: Canterbury Press.

Ross, C. and Baker, J., 2015. *Pioneering Spirituality: Resources for Reflection and Practice*. Norwich: Canterbury Press.

Ross, C. and Bevans, S., 2015. *Mission on the Road to Emmaus*. London: SCM Press.

Ross, C. and Smith, C., 2018. *Missional Conversations*. London: SCM.

Sadgrove, M., 2008. *Wisdom and Ministry*. London: SPCK.

Scott, S. P., 2006. *Redefining Small Churches – Exploring Issues of Survival and Change*. Unpublished MPhil. thesis, Partnership for Theological Education, University of Manchester.

Sell, A. P., 2014. *One Ministry, Many Ministers*. Eugene, Oregon: Pickwick Publications Wipf and Stock.

Skinner, F., 2020. *How to Enjoy Poetry (Little Ways to Live a Big Life)*. London: Quercus Publishing.

Slee, N., 2019. *Sabbath: The Hidden Heartbeat of our Lives*. London: Darton, Longman and Todd.

Smith, S., ed. May, W., 2015. *The Collected Poems and Drawings of Stevie Smith*. London: Faber and Faber Ltd.

Tucker, T., 2003. *Reformed Ministry: Traditions of Ministry and Ordination in the United Reformed Church*. London: United Reformed Church.

United Reformed Church, 1982. *Preparing Today for Tomorrow's Ministry*. London: United Reformed Church.

United Reformed Church, 1982. *Record of Assembly 1982*. London: United Reformed Church.

United Reformed Church, 1995. *Annual Reports, Resolutions and Papers 1995*. London: United Reformed Church.

United Reformed Church, 1995. *Assembly Record 1995*. London: United Reformed Church.

United Reformed Church, 2004. *Annual Reports, Resolutions and Papers 2004*. London: United Reformed Church.

United Reformed Church, 2004. *Assembly Record 2004*. London: United Reformed Church.

United Reformed Church, 2005. *Annual Reports, Resolutions and Papers 2005*. London: United Reformed Church.

United Reformed Church, 2006. *Annual Reports, Resolutions and Papers 2006*. London: United Reformed Church.

United Reformed Church, 2006. *Record of Assembly 2006.* London: United Reformed Church.

United Reformed Church, 2007. *Annual Reports, Resolutions and Papers 2007,* London: United Reformed Church.

United Reformed Church, 2007. *Record of the 2007 General Assembly.* London: United Reformed Church.

United Reformed Church, 2008. *Annual Reports, Resolutions and Papers 2008,* London: United Reformed Church.

United Reformed Church, 2008. *General Assembly 2008 Record.* London: United Reformed Church.

United Reformed Church, 2012. *Book of Reports 2012.* London: United Reformed Church.

United Reformed Church, 2012. *Renewing Reformed Theology.* London, United Reformed Church.

United Reformed Church, 2012. *United Reformed Church Record 2012.* London: United Reformed Church.

United Reformed Church, 2014. *Book of Reports 2014.* London: United Reformed Church.

United Reformed Church, 2016. *Book of Reports 2016.* London: United Reformed Church.

Valerio, R., Hodson, M. R., Hodson, M. J., Howles, T., 2020. *Covid-19 Environment, Justice and the Future.* Cambridge: Grove Books Ltd.

Vanstone, W. H., 1977. *Love's Endeavour, Love's Expense.* London: Darton, Longman and Todd Ltd.

Warner, M., Southgate, C., Grosch-Miller, C. A., Ison, H., 2020. *Tragedies and Christian Congregations.* Abingdon, Oxon: Routledge.

Williams, R., 2019. *Luminaries.* London: SPCK.

Williams, R., 2020. *Candles in the Dark Faith, Hope and Love in a Time of Pandemic.* London: SPCK.

Willimon, W. H. (ed.), 2002. *Pastor – A Reader for Ordained Ministry.* Nashville: Abingdon.

Wootton, J. (ed.), 2007. *This is Our Story.* Norwich: Epworth.

Wright, T., 2020. *God and the Pandemic.* London: SPCK.

WEBSITES AND DIGITAL DOCUMENTS

Aberdeen Presbytery, n.d. *Presbytery Plan.* [Online] Available at: http://www.aberdeenpresbytery.org.uk/latest-news/presbytery-plan/ [accessed 24th April 2020].

Alban at Duke Divinity School, n.d. *Alban Weekly.* [Online] Available at: https://alban.org/about-alban/alban-weekly/ [accessed 24th May 2021].

Alban Institute, 2017. *Alban Weekly.* [Online] Available at: https://alban.org/2017/06/22/r-alan-rice-the-demise-of-haystacks-and-the-future-of-the-rural-Church/ [accessed 24th April 2020].

Alban Institute, 2013. *The Small Church.* [Online] Available at: https://alban.org/archive/the-small-Church/ [accessed 24th April 2020].

Baines, Nick, 2021. *Thought for the Day.* [Online] Available at: https://nickbaines.wordpress.com/tag/thought-for-the-day/ [accessed 11th March 2021].

Ball, Peter, n.d. *A Pioneering God for a Pioneering People.* [Download] Available at: https://www.urc-eastern.org.uk/ tdo-local- Church/ focus-booklets /a-pioneering -god-for-a- pioneering-people/ [accessed 15th May 2020].

Black Country Radio, n.d. *Home.* [Online] Available at: http//www.blackcountryradio.co.uk [accessed 2nd April 2020].

Braithwaite, G., February 2020. *Church of England Church Buildings Council Struggling, Closed and Closing Churches Research Project Report.* [Online] Available at: https://www.churchofengland.org/sites/default/files/2020-02/Struggling_closed_and_closing_churches_report.pdf [accessed 4th November 2021].

Church Army, n.d. *Encounters on the Edge.* [Online] Available at: https://churcharmy.org/our-work/research/publications/encounters-on-the-edge/[accessed 29th March 2022].

Church Mission Society, n.d. *Pioneer Mission Leadership Training.* [Online] Available at: https://pioneer.Churchmissionsociety.org/ [accessed 24th April 2020].

Church Mission Society, 2022. *Newbigin Pioneering Hub.* [Online] Available at https://pioneer.churchmissionsociety.org/newbigin-pioneering-hub/ [accessed 15th July 2022].

Church Mission Society, n.d. *Pioneering Mission is a Spectrum.* [Online] Available at: https://Churchmissionsociety.org/resources/pioneering-mission-spectrum-tina-hodgett-paul-bradbury-anvil-vol-34-issue-1 [accessed 24th April 2020].

Crouch, A., Keilhacker, K. and Blanchard, D., n.d. *Leading Beyond the Blizzard.* [Online] Available at: https://journal.praxislabs.org/leading-beyond-the-blizzard-why-every-organization-is-now-a-startup-b7f32fb278ff [accessed 11th March 2021].

Empowering Design Practices, n.d. *Longitudinal Projects.* [Online] Available at: https://www.empoweringdesign.net/longitudinal-projects.html [accessed 24th April 2020].

Express and Star, 2017. *One Final Service at St John's in Stourbridge.* [Online] Available at: https://www.youtube.com/wv=sjynCrNpmjY [accessed 24th April 2020].

Fresh Expressions, n.d. *Fresh Expressions.* [Online] Available at: https://freshexpressions.org.uk/[accessed 24th April 2020].

Greenleaf, Robert K., n.d. *What is Servant Leadership?* Available at: https://www.greenleaf.org/what-is-servant-leadership/ [accessed 22nd May 2021].

Maxey, R., 2011. *Ruth's Blog.* [Online] Available at: https://ruthmaxey.wordpress.com/ [accessed 26th November 2019].

Praxislabs, n.d. Available at: https://www.praxislabs.org/ [accessed 23rd May 2021].

Roberto, J., n.d. *Guide to Transforming Faith Formation for a Changed World.* [Online] Available at: https://www.lifelongfaith.com/uploads/5/1/6/4/5164069/.pdf [accessed 11th March 2021].

Robson, J., n.d. *The Time has Come: Closing a Church Well in the Baptist Denomination.* [Online] Available at: https://baptisttimes.co.uk/Articles/495753/The_time_has.aspx [accessed 4th November 2021].

The Side by Side Theatre Company, Stourbridge, n.d. *The SideSpace at St John's.* [Online] Available at: http://thesidespace.org/ [accessed 24th April 2020].

Spencer, N., 2016. *Doing Good – a Future for Christianity in the 21st Century.* [Online] Available at: https://www.theosthinktank.co.uk/research/2016/12/14/doing-good-a-future-for-christianity-in-the-21st-century [accessed 24th May 2021].

Thorogood, Neil, 2011. *Westminster DNA.* [Online] Available via: https://www.neilthorogood.com/photo_9856828.html [accessed 26th November 2021].

Tragedy and Christian Congregations, n.d. [Online] Available at: https://tragedyandcongregations.org.uk/ [accessed 19th March 2021].

United Reformed Church, 2006. *Catch the Vision.* [Online] Available at: https://urc.org.uk/images/bltg/catch-the-vision-from-assembly_report_06.pdf [accessed 11th March 2021].

United Reformed Church, 2016. *What is the Spirit Saying to the Churches?* [Online] Available at: https://urc.org.uk/urc-resources/faith-and-order/2572-what-is-the-spirit-saying-to-the-Churches.html[accessed 24th April 2020].

United Reformed Church, 2016. *Book of Reports Southport Convention Centre 8th to 11th July 2016.* [Online] Available at: https://urc.org.uk/images/General-Assemblies/Assembly2016/assembly_reports_16.pdf [accessed 18th March 2021].

United Reformed Church, 2016. *Record General Assembly,*

Southport 2016. [Online] Available at: https://./urc.org.uk/images/General-Assemblies/Assembly2016/RECORD-2016w.pdf [accessed 18th March 2021].

United Reformed Church, 2021. *Church Life Review.* [Online] Available at https://urc.org.uk/wp-content/uploads/1638/27/Paper_N2_-_Church_Life_Review.pdf [accessed 15th July 2022].

United Reformed Church, 2021. *Future of the Church.* [Online] Available at https://urc.org.uk/images/MissionCouncil/March-2021/A1_Future_of_the_URC.pdf [accessed 15th July 2022]

United Reformed Church, 2022. *Newbigin Pioneering Hub.* [Online] Available at https://urc.org.uk/your-faith/more-about-ministry/newbigin-pioneering-hub/ [accessed 15th July 2022].

United Reformed Church, n.d. *Appreciating Church.* [Online] Available at: https://urc.org.uk/latest-news/2310-appreciating-Church-book-and-website-launch.html [accessed 11th March 2021].

United Reformed Church, n.d. *General Assembly Archive.* [Online] Available at: https://urc.org.uk/general-assembly/1158-general-assembly-archive.html [accessed 11th March 2021].

United Reformed Church, n.d. *Stepwise.* [Online] Available at: https://urc.org.uk/stepwise.html [accessed 22nd May 2021].

United Reformed Church, n.d. *The Manual.* [Online] Available at: https://urc.org.uk/images/the_manual/A_The_Basis_of_union_23_01_2020.pdf [accessed 24th April 2020]. Available at: https://urc.org.uk/images/the_manual/B-The_Manual_-_Section_B-2019.pdf [accessed 19th March 2021].

United Reformed Church, n.d. *Today's Daily Devotion.* [Online] Available at: https://devotions.urc.org.uk/todays-daily-devotion/ [accessed 30th November 2020].

United Reformed Church, n.d. *Walking the Way: Living the Life of Jesus Today.* [Online] Available at: https://urc.org.uk/our-work/walking-the-way.html [accessed 11th March 2021].

West Midlands Synod, n.d. *Worship in Lock-down.* [Online] Available at: https://www.youtube.com/watch?v=R0JgqhXcT68 [accessed 11th March 2021].

BIBLIOGRAPHY

This book is printed on paper from sustainable sources managed under the Forest Stewardship Council (FSC) scheme.

It has been printed in the UK to reduce transportation miles and their impact upon the environment.

For every new title that Matador publishes, we plant a tree to offset CO_2, partnering with the More Trees scheme.

For more about how Matador offsets its environmental impact, see www.troubador.co.uk/about/